Coding with Artificial Intelligence:

Unlocking the Future of Software Development with
Intelligent Automation, Machine Learning, and
Advanced AI Techniques"

Matthew D.Passmore

1

Table of Contents

Chapter 3.

Intelligent Code Completion

Predicting and Suggesting Code

Streamlining the Development Process

Empowering Developers of All Levels

Ensuring Accuracy and Contextual Relevance

Chapter 4.

Automated Code Review and Testing

Enhancing Code Quality Assurance.

Identifying and Fixing Bugs Early

Accelerating the Testing Process

Improving Collaboration and Communication

Chapter 5.

AI-Driven Debugging and Troubleshooting

Pinpointing and Resolving Issues

Minimizing Downtime and Disruptions

The Future of AI in Software Development

The Potential for Innovation and Growth
The Importance of Ethical Considerations
The Need for Continuous Learning and Adaptation
Embracing the AI-Powered Future

Chapter 1

Introduction

In the fast-paced world of software development, where innovation is the driving force and efficiency is paramount, Artificial Intelligence (AI) has emerged as a game-changer. AI is revolutionizing the way we build software, enabling intelligent automation, machine learning-powered insights, and advanced techniques that are unlocking unprecedented levels of productivity, quality, and creativity.

From automating repetitive tasks to generating code with remarkable accuracy, AI is transforming the software development landscape. Intelligent code completion, automated testing, and AI-driven debugging are streamlining the development process, empowering developers to focus on higher-level tasks and deliver exceptional results.

Machine learning algorithms are optimizing software performance, enhancing user experiences, and driving continuous improvement. Advanced AI techniques like natural language processing and computer vision are opening new frontiers for innovation, enabling developers to create more intuitive, intelligent, and impactful applications.

In this exploration of "Coding with Artificial Intelligence," we will delve into the exciting possibilities and transformative potential of AI in software development. We will uncover how AI is empowering developers, driving innovation, and shaping the future of software creation. Join us on this journey as we unlock the power of intelligent automation, machine learning, and advanced AI techniques to build a brighter, more efficient, and more impactful future for software development.

The Rise of AI in Software Development

In the ever-evolving realm of software development, a new era has dawned—an era where Artificial Intelligence (AI) is not just a buzzword, but a transformative force reshaping the very foundations of how we build software. The rise of AI in software development signifies a paradigm shift, where intelligent automation, machine learning insights, and advanced techniques are converging to redefine the boundaries of what's possible.

From Automation to Augmentation

Traditionally, software development was a labor-intensive process, demanding countless hours of manual coding, testing, and debugging. However, the advent of AI has ushered in a wave of automation, liberating developers from repetitive tasks and enabling them to focus on higher-level problem-solving and innovation.

AI-powered tools are now capable of generating code snippets, automating testing procedures, and even assisting in debugging, thereby accelerating development cycles and enhancing productivity. But AI's role isn't confined to mere automation; it's about augmentation—empowering developers with intelligent tools that amplify their capabilities and enable them to tackle more complex challenges.

Machine Learning: The Catalyst for Innovation

Machine Learning, a subset of AI, has emerged as a catalyst for innovation in software development. By analyzing vast amounts of data, machine learning algorithms can identify patterns, make predictions, and generate insights that inform decision-making and drive continuous improvement.

From optimizing code performance to personalizing user experiences, machine learning is enabling developers to create more intelligent, responsive, and user-centric applications. It's also revolutionizing the way we approach software testing and quality assurance, allowing for more efficient and effective identification and resolution of bugs.

Advanced AI Techniques: Pioneering New Frontiers

Beyond automation and machine learning, advanced AI techniques like natural language processing (NLP), computer vision, and deep learning are opening up new frontiers for software development. NLP enables applications to understand and interact with human language, paving the way for more intuitive and conversational user interfaces. Computer vision empowers software to interpret and understand visual information, unlocking a world of possibilities in areas like image recognition and augmented reality.

Deep learning, with its ability to model complex patterns and relationships, is driving breakthroughs in areas such as natural language understanding, machine translation, and even code generation itself.

The Future is Intelligent

The rise of AI in software development is not just a trend; it's a fundamental shift that's here to stay. As AI continues to evolve and mature, we can anticipate even more profound transformations in the way we build software. The future of software development is intelligent—a future where AI-powered tools and techniques empower developers to create more innovative, efficient, and impactful solutions.

In the following sections, we'll explore the specific ways in which AI is revolutionizing software development, from code generation and intelligent code completion to automated testing and AI-driven debugging. We'll delve into the applications of machine learning for software optimization and the potential of advanced AI techniques to shape the future of software creation. Join us on this exciting journey as we unlock the potential of AI to transform the world of software development.

The Power of Intelligent Automation

In the realm of software development, where efficiency and productivity reign supreme, intelligent automation has emerged as a transformative force. It's more than just automating repetitive tasks; it's about harnessing the power of AI to streamline workflows, optimize processes, and empower developers to focus on what truly matters: innovation and problem-solving.

Beyond Simple Automation

Traditional automation tools have long been used in software development to handle mundane and repetitive tasks, such as code compilation and deployment. However, intelligent automation takes this concept to the next level by infusing AI capabilities into the automation process. This allows for more sophisticated and adaptive automation that can handle complex scenarios and make intelligent decisions.

For instance, AI-powered automation tools can analyze code patterns, identify potential errors, and even suggest fixes, all without human intervention. This not only saves developers valuable time but also ensures higher code quality and consistency.

Streamlining Workflows

One of the key benefits of intelligent automation is its ability to streamline workflows across the entire software development lifecycle. From requirements gathering to deployment and maintenance, intelligent automation can orchestrate and optimize various tasks, reducing manual effort and minimizing errors.

For example, AI-powered tools can automate the creation of test cases based on requirements, execute those tests, and generate comprehensive reports, all with minimal human oversight. This accelerates the testing process and allows developers to identify and address issues early on, saving time and resources.

Empowering Developers

Intelligent automation isn't about replacing developers; it's about empowering them to focus on higher-value activities. By automating routine and repetitive tasks, developers can dedicate more time to creative problem-solving, designing innovative solutions, and improving user experiences.

Moreover, intelligent automation can provide developers with real-time insights and recommendations, enabling them to make informed decisions and optimize their code. This not only improves the quality of the software but also enhances the overall development experience.

Key Applications of Intelligent Automation in Software Development:

Code Generation: AI-powered tools can generate code snippets, templates, and even entire modules based on requirements and specifications, significantly speeding up development.

Testing and Quality Assurance: Automated testing tools can execute test cases, analyze results, and identify defects, ensuring software quality and reliability.

Deployment and DevOps: Intelligent automation can streamline the deployment process, automate infrastructure provisioning, and enable continuous integration and continuous delivery (CI/CD).

Maintenance and Support: AI-powered tools can monitor applications, identify performance issues, and suggest optimizations, ensuring smooth operation and user satisfaction.

Embracing the Future

The power of intelligent automation in software development is undeniable. It's transforming the way we build software, enabling greater efficiency, productivity, and innovation. As AI continues to advance, we can expect even more sophisticated and impactful automation capabilities that will further revolutionize the software development landscape.

By embracing intelligent automation, developers can unlock new levels of productivity, creativity, and success. It's not just about working faster; it's about working smarter and focusing on what truly matters: creating exceptional software that meets the evolving needs of users and businesses.

The Impact of Machine Learning

Machine Learning (ML), a subset of AI that focuses on enabling systems to learn from data and improve their performance without being explicitly programmed, is wielding a profound impact on the software development landscape. Its ability to analyze vast datasets, identify patterns, and make predictions is revolutionizing various aspects of the development process, from code generation to testing and optimization.

Enhanced Code Generation and Completion

ML algorithms are empowering code generation tools to go beyond simple templates and automate the creation of complex code structures based on requirements and specifications. By learning from existing codebases and developer behavior, ML models can predict and suggest code snippets, entire functions, or even complete modules, significantly accelerating development and reducing errors.

Moreover, ML-powered code completion tools are becoming increasingly sophisticated, offering contextually relevant and accurate suggestions that enhance developer productivity and ensure code consistency.

Intelligent Testing and Quality Assurance

ML is transforming the way we approach software testing and quality assurance. By analyzing historical test data and code patterns, ML algorithms can identify potential areas of risk and generate test cases that are more likely to uncover defects. This targeted approach to testing not only saves time and resources but also improves the effectiveness of quality assurance efforts.

Furthermore, ML-powered tools can analyze code during development, flagging potential errors and vulnerabilities before they become critical issues. This proactive approach to bug detection helps prevent costly delays and ensures software reliability.

Data-Driven Insights and Optimization

One of the most significant impacts of ML is its ability to provide developers with data-driven insights into software performance, user behavior, and potential issues. By analyzing large volumes of data generated by applications, ML algorithms can identify performance bottlenecks, predict user preferences, and uncover hidden patterns that can inform design decisions and optimization efforts.

This data-driven approach to software development enables developers to create more efficient, responsive, and user-centric applications that deliver exceptional experiences.

Predictive Analytics and Proactive Problem-Solving

ML's predictive capabilities are also revolutionizing software maintenance and support. By analyzing historical data and identifying patterns, ML algorithms can predict potential issues and failures before they occur, allowing for proactive problem-solving and minimizing downtime.

This predictive approach to maintenance not only enhances software reliability and stability but also improves user satisfaction by preventing disruptions and ensuring smooth operation.

Conclusion

The impact of machine learning on software development is far-reaching and transformative. It's enabling developers to create more intelligent, efficient, and user-centric applications while streamlining the development process and improving software quality.

As ML continues to advance and integrate further into the software development lifecycle, we can expect even more exciting innovations and breakthroughs that will reshape the way we build software and deliver exceptional experiences. The future of software development is undoubtedly intertwined with the power of machine learning, and its potential to drive innovation and progress is limitless.

Exploring Advanced AI Techniques

NLP focuses on enabling computers to understand, interpret, and generate human language. In software development, NLP is revolutionizing the way we interact with applications, paving the way for more natural and conversational user interfaces.

Chatbots, virtual assistants, and voice-activated commands are just a few examples of how NLP is transforming the user experience. By understanding and responding to natural language queries, these applications make technology more accessible and intuitive, bridging the gap between humans and machines.

Computer Vision: Empowering Software to "See"

Computer Vision equips software with the ability to interpret and understand visual information from the world around us. This powerful technique is driving innovation in various areas of software development, including:

Image Recognition: From facial recognition in security systems to object detection in autonomous vehicles, computer vision is enabling software to identify and classify objects in images and videos with remarkable accuracy.

Augmented Reality: By overlaying digital information onto the real world, computer vision is powering immersive augmented reality experiences that enhance user engagement and interaction.

Quality Assurance: Computer vision can be used to automate visual inspection tasks, ensuring product quality and consistency in manufacturing and other industries.

Deep Learning: Unleashing the Power of Neural Networks

Deep Learning, a subset of machine learning that utilizes artificial neural networks, is driving breakthroughs in various areas of software development. Its ability to model complex patterns and relationships in data is enabling advancements in:

Natural Language Understanding: Deep learning models are improving machine translation, sentiment analysis, and other NLP tasks, enabling more accurate and nuanced understanding of human language.

Image and Video Analysis: Deep learning is powering advancements in image recognition, object detection, and video analysis, leading to innovations in areas like autonomous vehicles, medical imaging, and surveillance systems.

Code Generation: Deep learning models are being explored for generating code snippets and even entire programs based on requirements and specifications, potentially revolutionizing the development process.

Reinforcement Learning: Learning from Experience

Reinforcement Learning focuses on enabling software agents to learn through trial and error, receiving rewards or penalties based on their actions. This technique is particularly promising in areas such as:

Game Development: Reinforcement learning has been used to train agents that can play complex games at superhuman levels, pushing the boundaries of AI and game design.

Robotics: By learning from their interactions with the environment, reinforcement learning algorithms can enable robots to perform complex tasks and adapt to new situations.

Optimization: Reinforcement learning can be applied to optimize complex systems and processes, improving efficiency and performance.

The Future of Advanced AI Techniques

As AI continues to evolve, we can expect even more groundbreaking advancements in these advanced techniques and the emergence of new ones. The potential for innovation and transformation in software development is immense.

By embracing these advanced AI techniques, developers can create more intelligent, intuitive, and impactful applications that solve complex problems, enhance user experiences, and drive progress in various industries. The future of software development is undoubtedly intertwined with the power of advanced AI, and its potential to shape the world around us is limitless.

Chapter 2.

AI-Powered Code Generation

In the realm of software development, where time is of the essence and innovation is paramount, AI-powered code generation is emerging as a game-changer. By leveraging the power of machine learning and advanced algorithms, AI is automating the creation of code, enabling developers to work faster, smarter, and more creatively.

Automating the Tedious

Traditionally, code generation has involved manually writing lines of code, a process that can be time-consuming and prone to errors. AI-powered code generation tools are changing this paradigm by automating the creation of code snippets, functions, and even entire modules based on requirements, specifications, and natural language descriptions.

This automation not only saves developers valuable time but also reduces the likelihood of errors and inconsistencies, leading to more reliable and maintainable code.

Boosting Productivity and Efficiency

One of the most significant benefits of AI-powered code generation is its ability to boost productivity and efficiency. By automating repetitive coding tasks, developers can focus on higher-level problem-solving, design, and innovation.

Moreover, AI code generation tools can suggest optimizations and best practices, helping developers write cleaner, more efficient code that performs better and consumes fewer resources.

Enhancing Code Quality and Consistency

AI-powered code generation tools are trained on vast datasets of high-quality code, enabling them to generate code that adheres to industry standards and best practices. This ensures consistency across projects and reduces the likelihood of introducing bugs and vulnerabilities.

Furthermore, these tools can analyze code for potential errors, security flaws, and performance bottlenecks, providing developers with valuable insights and recommendations for improvement.

Overcoming Challenges and Limitations

While AI-powered code generation holds immense promise, it's important to acknowledge the challenges and limitations.

Complexity: Generating complex code structures and algorithms can still be challenging for AI, requiring careful design and validation.
Context: AI models may struggle to understand the broader context of a project, leading to code that doesn't integrate seamlessly.

Creativity: While AI can automate code generation, it may not fully replace the creativity and intuition of human developers in certain scenarios.

The Future of AI-Powered Code Generation

Despite these challenges, the future of AI-powered code generation is bright. As AI models become more sophisticated and capable of understanding complex requirements and contexts, they will play an increasingly important role in software development.

We can anticipate:

More Powerful Code Generation: AI will generate increasingly complex and nuanced code structures, handling more intricate tasks and scenarios.

Improved Contextual Understanding: AI models will better grasp the broader context of projects, leading to more seamless code integration.

Collaboration: AI and human developers will collaborate more effectively, with AI automating routine tasks and providing insights while humans focus on creativity and problem-solving.

Conclusion

AI-powered code generation is revolutionizing software development, enabling developers to work faster, smarter, and more creatively. By automating tedious tasks, boosting productivity, and enhancing code quality, AI is empowering developers to build better software and deliver exceptional results.

As AI continues to advance, we can expect code generation tools to become even more powerful and versatile, playing an increasingly integral role in the software development lifecycle. The future of coding is undoubtedly intertwined with the power of AI, and its potential to transform the industry is limitless.

Automating Code Creation

In the fast-paced world of software development, automating code creation through AI has emerged as a transformative force. By leveraging machine learning and advanced algorithms, AI is automating the generation of code snippets, functions, and even entire modules, revolutionizing how developers work and accelerating the development process.

From Manual Labor to Intelligent Automation

Traditionally, code creation has been a labor-intensive process, requiring developers to manually write each line of code. This approach can be time-consuming, prone to errors, and often hinders productivity. AI-powered code automation tools are changing this paradigm by automating the generation of code based on requirements, specifications, and even natural language descriptions.

This automation not only saves developers valuable time but also reduces the likelihood of errors and inconsistencies, leading to more reliable and maintainable code.

Empowering Developers to Focus on Innovation

One of the key benefits of automating code creation is its ability to free developers from repetitive and mundane tasks. By automating the generation of boilerplate code, data structures, and other common elements, developers can focus their energy and expertise on higher-level problem-solving, design, and innovation.

This shift in focus allows developers to be more creative and strategic, ultimately leading to the development of more sophisticated and impactful software solutions.

Accelerating the Development Process

Automating code creation significantly accelerates the development process. By generating code rapidly and accurately, developers can iterate faster, experiment with new ideas, and bring products to market sooner.

This increased speed and agility can be a competitive advantage in today's fast-paced business environment, where time-to-market is often critical.

Improving Code Quality and Consistency

AI-powered code automation tools are trained on vast datasets of high-quality code, enabling them to generate code that adheres to industry standards and best practices. This ensures consistency across projects and reduces the likelihood of introducing bugs and vulnerabilities.

Furthermore, these tools can analyze code for potential errors, security flaws, and performance bottlenecks, providing developers with valuable insights and recommendations for improvement.

How to Create Code with AI

Here's a simplified breakdown of how to generate code using AI tools:

Choose an AI Code Generation Tool: Several AI-powered code generation tools are available, such as GitHub Copilot, Tabnine, and CodeT5. Select one that suits your programming language and development environment.

Provide Input: Depending on the tool, you can provide input in various ways:

Natural Language Descriptions: Describe the functionality you want to achieve in plain English.
Code Comments: Write comments within your code to specify the desired code behavior.
Partial Code: Start writing code, and the AI will suggest completions and generate the remaining parts.
Review and Refine: The AI will generate code suggestions or complete code snippets. Review the generated code carefully, ensuring it meets your requirements and adheres to best practices. Refine the code as needed.

Integrate and Test: Integrate the generated code into your project and thoroughly test it to ensure it functions correctly and integrates seamlessly with the rest of your codebase.

Important Considerations:

AI is a Tool, Not a Replacement: AI code generation tools are powerful assistants, but they are not a replacement for human developers. Human oversight, critical thinking, and problem-solving skills remain crucial for successful software development.

Understand the Limitations: AI models may have limitations in understanding complex requirements or generating code for highly specialized domains. Be aware of these limitations and use AI tools judiciously.

Security: Always review AI-generated code for potential security vulnerabilities before integrating it into your project.

The Future of Automated Code Creation

As AI continues to advance, we can expect code automation tools to become even more powerful and versatile. They will be able to handle more complex scenarios, understand natural language instructions more accurately, and generate code that is increasingly optimized and efficient.

In the future, we can envision a world where developers collaborate seamlessly with AI, leveraging its capabilities to automate routine tasks and focus on the creative and strategic aspects of software development.

Conclusion

Automating code creation through AI is revolutionizing the software development landscape. It is empowering developers to work faster, smarter, and more creatively, ultimately leading to the development of more innovative, reliable, and impactful software solutions.

By embracing the power of AI-powered code automation, developers can unlock new levels of productivity, efficiency, and innovation, propelling the software industry into a future of unprecedented possibilities.

Boosting Productivity and Efficiency

In the fast-paced and demanding world of software development, time is a precious commodity. AI-powered tools and techniques are revolutionizing productivity and efficiency by automating mundane tasks, streamlining workflows, and empowering developers to focus on innovation and problem-solving.

Accelerating Development Cycles

AI-driven automation significantly speeds up various stages of the software development lifecycle. Code generation tools can quickly produce boilerplate code, saving developers countless hours of manual typing. Automated testing frameworks can execute test cases rapidly and efficiently, reducing the time required for quality assurance. AI-powered deployment tools streamline the process of releasing software updates, minimizing downtime and ensuring seamless transitions.

Enhancing Developer Focus

By automating repetitive and time-consuming tasks, AI frees developers from mundane chores, allowing them to dedicate their expertise to higher-value activities. They can focus on designing creative solutions, refining user experiences, and tackling complex challenges that require critical thinking and problem-solving skills. This shift in focus empowers developers to reach their full potential and deliver exceptional results.

Streamlining Collaboration and Communication

AI-powered tools facilitate seamless collaboration and communication within development teams. Code review platforms leverage AI to analyze code changes, identify potential errors, and suggest improvements, fostering knowledge sharing and ensuring code quality. Project management tools utilize AI to track progress, allocate resources, and identify potential bottlenecks, enabling teams to stay organized and on track.

Optimizing Resource Allocation

AI helps optimize resource allocation by analyzing project requirements, developer skillsets, and available resources. This intelligent allocation ensures that the right people are working on the right tasks at the right time, maximizing productivity and minimizing waste.

Enabling Continuous Learning and Improvement

AI-powered analytics tools provide valuable insights into developer performance, code quality, and project efficiency. By identifying areas for improvement and suggesting best practices, AI fosters a culture of continuous learning and helps developers enhance their skills and knowledge.

Real-World Examples

Several real-world examples demonstrate how AI is boosting productivity and efficiency in software development:

GitHub Copilot: This AI-powered code completion tool suggests code snippets and even entire functions based on context, helping developers write code faster and with fewer errors.

DeepCode: This AI-powered code review platform analyzes code for potential bugs, security vulnerabilities, and performance issues, streamlining the code review process and improving code quality.

Jenkins: This popular automation server utilizes AI to orchestrate and automate various stages of the software development pipeline, enabling continuous integration and delivery.

Conclusion

The impact of AI on productivity and efficiency in software development is undeniable. By automating tasks, streamlining workflows, and empowering developers, AI is transforming the way software is built, enabling faster development cycles, improved code quality, and enhanced collaboration.

As AI continues to evolve, we can expect even more powerful tools and techniques that will further boost productivity and efficiency. Embracing AI is no longer a luxury but a necessity for software development teams looking to stay ahead in today's competitive landscape.

Enhancing Code Quality and Consistency

In the realm of software development, where reliability and maintainability are paramount, AI is emerging as a powerful ally in enhancing code quality and consistency. Through intelligent analysis, automation, and insightful recommendations, AI-powered tools are transforming the way developers write, review, and maintain code, ultimately leading to more robust and resilient software solutions.

Static Code Analysis and Automated Reviews

AI-driven static code analysis tools can scan codebases for potential errors, bugs, security vulnerabilities, and performance bottlenecks. These tools go beyond simple syntax checks, leveraging machine learning algorithms to identify patterns and anomalies that may indicate underlying issues. By automating code reviews, developers can catch errors early in the development cycle, preventing costly rework and ensuring code adheres to best practices and coding standards.

Intelligent Code Completion and Refactoring

AI-powered code completion tools offer context-aware suggestions and even generate entire code snippets, helping developers write code faster and with fewer errors. These tools learn from vast code repositories and developer behavior, providing intelligent recommendations that align with project conventions and coding styles. Additionally, AI-driven refactoring tools can suggest improvements to existing code, making it more readable, maintainable, and efficient.

Test Case Generation and Automated Testing

AI can automate the generation of test cases based on code analysis and requirements, ensuring comprehensive test coverage and reducing the risk of overlooking critical scenarios. AI-powered testing frameworks can execute these test cases efficiently, identifying potential issues and regressions early in the development process. This proactive approach to testing helps prevent bugs from reaching production and ensures software reliability.

Continuous Integration and Continuous Delivery (CI/CD)

AI-powered CI/CD pipelines automate the build, test, and deployment processes, ensuring code changes are integrated and delivered seamlessly and frequently. This approach enables faster feedback loops, reduces the risk of integration issues, and allows for more rapid and reliable software releases.

Real-World Examples

Several real-world examples showcase how AI is enhancing code quality and consistency:

DeepCode: This AI-powered code review platform analyzes code for potential security vulnerabilities, bugs, and performance issues, providing developers with actionable insights to improve code quality.

SonarQube: This open-source platform leverages AI to analyze code quality, identify technical debt, and track code smells, helping developers maintain clean and maintainable codebases.

Codacy: This AI-powered code quality platform automates code reviews, identifies security issues, and provides code style recommendations, ensuring code consistency and adherence to best practices.

Conclusion

AI is playing a pivotal role in enhancing code quality and consistency, empowering developers to write cleaner, more reliable, and more maintainable code. By automating code reviews, suggesting improvements, and facilitating seamless integration and delivery, AI-powered tools are elevating software standards and contributing to the development of more robust and resilient applications.

Embracing AI in the pursuit of code quality and consistency is not just a best practice; it's a strategic imperative for development teams looking to deliver exceptional software that meets the evolving needs of users and businesses. As AI continues to advance, we can anticipate even more sophisticated tools and techniques that will further empower developers to write code that is not only functional but also elegant, efficient, and secure.

Overcoming Challenges and Limitations

While AI-powered code generation holds immense promise for revolutionizing software development, it's essential to acknowledge and address its challenges and limitations to harness its full potential. By understanding these hurdles and implementing strategies to overcome them, developers can ensure the successful adoption and integration of AI code generation into their workflows.

Complexity and Contextual Understanding

One of the primary challenges lies in generating complex code structures and algorithms that accurately reflect project requirements and integrate seamlessly with existing codebases. AI models may struggle to grasp the broader context and intricacies of a project, potentially leading to code that is functionally correct but lacks proper integration or fails to address edge cases.

To overcome this, developers can provide clear and detailed instructions, including specific examples and use cases, to guide the AI's code generation.

Additionally, leveraging techniques like fine-tuning pre-trained models on project-specific data can help improve the AI's contextual understanding and generate more relevant code.

Accuracy and Reliability

Ensuring the accuracy and reliability of AI-generated code is crucial. While AI models are trained on vast datasets, they may still produce code with errors, inconsistencies, or security vulnerabilities.

Thorough code review and testing remain essential, even with AI-generated code. Developers should carefully scrutinize the output, validate its functionality, and address any potential issues before integration. Incorporating automated testing and code analysis tools can further enhance the reliability of AI-generated code.

Creativity and Innovation

While AI excels at automating routine tasks and generating code based on patterns, it may not fully replicate the creativity and intuition of human developers in certain scenarios. AI models may struggle to generate truly innovative or unconventional solutions that push the boundaries of software development.

To address this, developers should view AI as a powerful assistant rather than a replacement for human ingenuity. By leveraging AI to handle repetitive tasks and provide insights, developers can free up their time and mental energy to focus on creative problem-solving and exploring new ideas.

Bias and Ethical Considerations

AI models are trained on existing codebases, which may inadvertently contain biases or reflect historical practices that are no longer relevant or appropriate. It's essential to be aware of potential biases in AI-generated code and ensure that it adheres to ethical and inclusive standards.

Regularly evaluating and updating training data, as well as incorporating diverse perspectives in the development and deployment of AI code generation tools, can help mitigate bias and promote fairness.

Conclusion

AI-powered code generation is a rapidly evolving field with immense potential. By acknowledging and addressing its challenges and limitations, developers can successfully harness its power to accelerate development, improve code quality, and foster innovation.

The key lies in viewing AI as a collaborative tool that complements human expertise. By working in tandem with AI, developers can leverage its strengths while mitigating its limitations, ultimately leading to a more productive, efficient, and creative software development process.

Chapter 3.

Intelligent Code Completion

Intelligent code completion represents a significant advancement in the way developers write code. By leveraging AI and machine learning algorithms, these tools analyze context, predict intentions, and offer contextually relevant code suggestions, transforming the coding experience from a manual task into a collaborative journey with an AI assistant.

Contextual Awareness and Predictive Capabilities

Unlike traditional code completion tools that rely on simple syntax matching, intelligent code completion tools analyze the surrounding code, project structure, and even developer coding patterns to provide suggestions that are more accurate, relevant, and insightful.

These tools understand the context in which you're coding, allowing them to predict the most likely next steps and offer suggestions that accelerate development and reduce errors. They may suggest variable names, function calls, method implementations, or even entire code blocks, saving developers valuable time and mental effort.

Empowering Developers of All Levels

Intelligent code completion tools benefit developers of all skill levels. For beginners, these tools act as helpful guides, offering suggestions that help them learn coding conventions and best practices. For experienced developers, these tools streamline workflows, automate repetitive tasks, and enhance productivity, allowing them to focus on more complex and creative challenges.

Seamless Integration and Customization

Intelligent code completion tools are often seamlessly integrated into popular code editors and IDEs, providing a frictionless and intuitive user experience. They are also highly customizable, allowing developers to tailor the suggestions to their specific needs and preferences.

The Benefits of Intelligent Code Completion

Increased productivity: By automating code suggestions and completions, developers can write code faster and with fewer errors.

Improved code quality: Intelligent suggestions help developers adhere to coding standards and best practices, leading to more reliable and maintainable code.

Enhanced learning: These tools offer valuable insights and suggestions that help developers learn and grow their coding skills.

Reduced cognitive load: By automating routine tasks, developers can focus on higher-level problem-solving and innovation.

The Future of Intelligent Code Completion

As AI and machine learning continue to advance, intelligent code completion tools will become even more sophisticated and powerful. We can anticipate:

Even more accurate and contextually relevant suggestions: AI models will become better at understanding code context and developer intentions, offering even more precise and helpful suggestions.

Personalized recommendations: Tools will adapt to individual coding styles and preferences, providing tailored suggestions that improve workflow and efficiency.

Multi-language support: AI models will support a wider range of programming languages, making intelligent code completion accessible to even more developers.

Conclusion

Intelligent code completion represents a significant leap forward in developer productivity and code quality. By harnessing the power of AI and machine learning, these tools empower developers to write code faster, smarter, and with greater confidence.

As the technology continues to evolve, we can expect even more exciting innovations and breakthroughs that will further transform the coding landscape.

Predicting and Suggesting Code

In the realm of software development, where every keystroke counts, the ability to predict and suggest code is a game-changer. AI-powered code completion tools are revolutionizing the way developers write code, leveraging machine learning and advanced algorithms to anticipate developer intentions and offer contextually relevant suggestions.

Contextual Awareness and Predictive Capabilities

Unlike traditional code completion tools that rely on basic syntax matching, AI-powered tools analyze the surrounding code, project structure, and even developer coding patterns to provide more accurate and insightful suggestions.

These tools consider the current context, including the programming language, libraries being used, and the overall structure of the code. They can also learn from your coding style and preferences, offering suggestions that align with your unique approach. This level of contextual awareness allows AI models to predict what you're likely to type next and offer suggestions that streamline the coding process and reduce errors.

Streamlining the Development Process

By predicting and suggesting code, AI tools help developers write code faster and with fewer errors. Instead of manually typing out every character, developers can simply select from a list of relevant suggestions, accelerating the coding process and minimizing the risk of typos and syntax mistakes.

Moreover, AI code completion can offer suggestions for entire code blocks, functions, or even classes, further streamlining development and allowing developers to focus on higher-level tasks.

Empowering Developers of All Levels

AI-powered code completion tools benefit developers of all skill levels. For beginners, these tools act as helpful guides, offering suggestions that help them learn coding conventions and best practices. For experienced developers, these tools can automate repetitive tasks, enhance productivity, and offer insights into alternative approaches or optimized solutions.

Ensuring Accuracy and Contextual Relevance

AI models are continuously learning and improving, striving to provide accurate and contextually relevant suggestions. They are trained on vast datasets of code, enabling them to identify patterns and understand common coding practices. However, it's important to remember that AI is not infallible.

Developers should always review and validate suggested code before accepting it, ensuring it aligns with their intentions and adheres to project requirements. The collaboration between human developers and AI tools is key to achieving optimal results.

Examples of AI-Powered Code Completion Tools:

GitHub Copilot: This powerful AI tool, trained on billions of lines of code, provides context-aware suggestions for entire lines or blocks of code, accelerating development and reducing errors.
Tabnine: This AI code completion tool offers suggestions based on context, code patterns, and even natural language descriptions, empowering developers to write code faster and with greater confidence.
Kite: This AI-powered coding assistant provides intelligent code completions, documentation lookups, and even code examples, helping developers learn and become more productive.

Conclusion

AI-powered code prediction and suggestion are transforming the coding landscape, making the development process faster, more efficient, and less error-prone. By leveraging the power of AI, developers can focus on innovation, problem-solving, and creating impactful software solutions, while leaving the mundane and repetitive tasks to their intelligent coding assistants.

As AI continues to evolve, we can anticipate even more sophisticated code completion tools that offer deeper contextual understanding, personalized recommendations, and support for a wider range of programming languages, further empowering developers and shaping the future of software development.

Streamlining the Development Process

In the world of software development, speed, efficiency, and agility are critical. AI is playing a pivotal role in streamlining the development process, enabling teams to deliver high-quality software faster and with fewer resources. By automating repetitive tasks, providing intelligent insights, and optimizing workflows, AI is transforming the way software is built, tested, and deployed.

Automation of Routine Tasks

AI-powered tools are automating a wide range of routine and repetitive tasks, freeing developers to focus on more strategic and creative aspects of the development process. Code generation, automated testing, and deployment orchestration are just a few examples of how AI is eliminating manual effort and reducing the potential for human errors.

Intelligent Code Completion and Refactoring

AI-powered code completion tools suggest code snippets, entire functions, and even refactor existing code based on context and best practices. This streamlines development, reduces errors, and ensures code consistency, allowing developers to focus on the logic and functionality of their applications.

Predictive Analytics and Early Issue Detection

AI can analyze historical data and code patterns to predict potential issues and vulnerabilities before they become critical problems. This proactive approach allows developers to address issues early in the development cycle, saving time and resources and preventing costly delays.

Optimized Testing and Quality Assurance

AI-powered testing tools can automatically generate and execute test cases, analyze test results, and identify defects with greater accuracy and efficiency. This streamlines the testing process, improves software quality, and reduces the time required for quality assurance.

Enhanced Collaboration and Communication

AI-powered tools facilitate seamless collaboration and communication among development teams. Code review platforms leverage AI to analyze code changes, identify potential issues, and suggest improvements, fostering knowledge sharing and ensuring code quality. Project management tools utilize AI to track progress, allocate resources, and identify potential bottlenecks, enabling teams to stay organized and on track.

Continuous Integration and Continuous Delivery (CI/CD)

AI-powered CI/CD pipelines automate the build, test, and deployment processes, enabling faster and more frequent software releases. This approach allows for continuous feedback and improvement, ensuring that software is always up-to-date and meets the evolving needs of users.

Real-World Examples

Microsoft's Visual Studio IntelliCode: This AI-powered tool provides intelligent code completions and suggestions based on context and best practices, helping developers write code faster and with fewer errors.

Google's Cloud AutoML: This platform enables developers to build custom machine learning models without extensive expertise, streamlining the process of incorporating AI into their applications.

Amazon CodeGuru: This AI-powered code review tool provides intelligent recommendations to improve code quality and identify potential issues.

Conclusion

AI is playing a crucial role in streamlining the development process, empowering teams to deliver high-quality software faster and more efficiently. By automating tasks, providing intelligent insights, and optimizing workflows, AI is transforming the way software is built, tested, and deployed.

Embracing AI in the development process is not just about keeping up with the latest trends; it's about unlocking new levels of productivity, efficiency, and innovation. As AI continues to evolve, we can expect even more powerful tools and techniques that will further streamline development and empower developers to create exceptional software solutions.

Empowering Developers of All Levels

One of the most remarkable aspects of AI-powered coding tools is their ability to empower developers across the entire spectrum of experience, from novices taking their first steps to seasoned professionals navigating complex projects. AI's inclusive nature democratizes access to advanced coding capabilities, leveling the playing field and fostering a more collaborative and supportive development environment.

For Beginners: A Guiding Hand and Accelerated Learning

For those new to coding, AI tools can act as a patient and knowledgeable mentor. Intelligent code completion and suggestion features offer real-time guidance, helping beginners understand syntax, conventions, and best practices. AI-powered debugging tools can identify and explain errors in a clear and concise manner, facilitating the learning process and building confidence. By automating repetitive tasks and providing helpful prompts, AI tools allow beginners to focus on grasping core concepts and building foundational skills, accelerating their journey towards proficiency.

For Intermediate Developers: Boosting Productivity and Confidence

AI tools provide intermediate developers with a valuable boost in productivity and efficiency. Code generation and automation features streamline workflows, reducing the time spent on mundane tasks and allowing for greater focus on problem-solving and innovation. Intelligent code completion and refactoring suggestions enhance code quality and maintainability, fostering good coding habits and professional development. AI-powered debugging tools expedite issue resolution, minimizing frustration and enabling developers to tackle more challenging projects with confidence.

For Experienced Developers: Unlocking New Possibilities

Even seasoned developers can benefit significantly from AI's capabilities. By automating routine tasks and providing insightful suggestions, AI tools free up valuable time for experienced developers to focus on complex problem-solving, architectural design, and exploring new technologies. AI-powered code analysis tools can identify potential performance bottlenecks or security vulnerabilities, helping experienced developers maintain high standards and deliver robust software solutions. Furthermore, AI can assist in exploring novel approaches and optimizing code for maximum efficiency, pushing the boundaries of innovation.

Collaboration and Knowledge Sharing

AI tools foster collaboration and knowledge sharing within development teams. Code reviews become more efficient and insightful with AI-powered analysis, allowing for constructive feedback and knowledge exchange among developers of varying experience levels. AI-driven project management tools promote transparency and coordination, enabling teams to work seamlessly and achieve shared goals.

Conclusion

AI is democratizing coding by empowering developers of all levels to achieve more, learn faster, and collaborate effectively. By providing intelligent assistance, automating tasks, and offering valuable insights, AI tools create an inclusive environment where everyone can contribute and grow.

As AI continues to advance, we can anticipate even more powerful tools and techniques that will further empower developers, regardless of their experience level, to create innovative, impactful, and accessible software solutions. The future of coding is one of collaboration, inclusivity, and boundless potential, driven by the transformative power of AI.

Ensuring Accuracy and Contextual Relevance

While the power of AI-powered code completion lies in its ability to predict and suggest code, ensuring the accuracy and contextual relevance of those suggestions is paramount. Developers rely on these tools to enhance productivity and streamline workflows, but inaccurate or irrelevant suggestions can lead to errors, confusion, and frustration. AI developers are constantly working to refine the underlying models and techniques to ensure code completion tools deliver the most helpful and accurate recommendations possible.

Contextual Understanding

The cornerstone of accurate and relevant code completion lies in a deep understanding of context. AI models must grasp the programming language being used, the libraries and frameworks involved, the project's specific structure, and the developer's coding style and intentions.

To achieve this, advanced techniques such as natural language processing (NLP) and deep learning are employed. NLP helps AI models interpret code comments, variable names, and surrounding code structures to infer meaning and context. Deep learning models, trained on massive code repositories, learn patterns and relationships in code, enabling them to make more informed predictions about the developer's next steps.

Continuous Learning and Adaptation

AI models are not static entities; they continually learn and adapt based on user interactions and feedback. Every time a developer accepts or rejects a suggestion, the AI model updates its understanding of context and intent. Over time, this leads to increasingly personalized and accurate suggestions that align with individual coding styles and project requirements.

User Feedback and Customization

Developers play a crucial role in ensuring accuracy and relevance by providing feedback on suggestions. Most AI code completion tools allow users to rate or comment on suggestions, helping the AI model refine its understanding and improve future recommendations. Additionally, customization options allow developers to tailor suggestions to their specific needs and preferences, further enhancing the relevance of the AI's output.

Hybrid Approaches

Some AI code completion tools employ hybrid approaches, combining AI models with static code analysis and other techniques to enhance accuracy and relevance. Static code analysis helps identify potential errors and inconsistencies in the code, providing additional context for the AI model to generate more informed suggestions.

Challenges and Future Directions

While significant progress has been made in ensuring accuracy and contextual relevance, challenges remain. AI models may still struggle in understanding complex or ambiguous scenarios, leading to less relevant suggestions. Additionally, biases in training data can impact the AI's understanding and lead to biased or inappropriate suggestions.

Ongoing research and development are focused on addressing these challenges and improving the accuracy and relevance of AI code completion. Advancements in natural language understanding, deeper contextual analysis, and more personalized models are expected to further enhance the capabilities of these tools.

Conclusion

Ensuring accuracy and contextual relevance in intelligent code completion is an ongoing journey, but the progress made so far is promising. By leveraging AI's ability to understand context, learn from user interactions, and adapt to individual preferences, developers can harness the full potential of code completion tools to streamline workflows, improve code quality, and focus on the creative aspects of software development.

As AI continues to advance, we can anticipate even more sophisticated and personalized code completion experiences that will further empower developers and shape the future of coding.

Sources and related content

How continuous-learning AI sharpens predictions - Algolia

www.algolia.com

Training Data Biases and Their Impact on AI Code Assistants' Generated Code | Blog | Digital.ai

digital.ai

Chapter 4.

Automated Code Review and Testing

In the realm of software development, ensuring code quality and reliability is paramount. Automated code review and testing, powered by AI, is revolutionizing the quality assurance process, enabling faster feedback loops, improved defect detection, and enhanced collaboration among development teams.

Automated Code Review: Catching Errors Early

AI-powered code review tools analyze code changes, identify potential errors, security vulnerabilities, and performance issues. These tools leverage static code analysis, machine learning algorithms, and vast code repositories to provide insightful feedback and recommendations. By automating code reviews, developers can catch errors early in the development cycle, preventing them from propagating and causing costly issues later.

Automated Testing: Ensuring Comprehensive Coverage

AI-powered testing frameworks can automatically generate and execute test cases based on code analysis, requirements, and user scenarios. This ensures comprehensive test coverage and reduces the risk of overlooking critical test cases. Automated testing also allows for faster and more frequent testing, enabling continuous integration and delivery (CI/CD) pipelines to operate seamlessly.

Accelerating Feedback Loops

Automated code review and testing provide rapid feedback to developers, enabling them to address issues promptly and iterate quickly. This accelerated feedback loop facilitates a more agile development process, where code changes are continuously integrated, tested, and refined.

Improving Collaboration

AI-powered tools facilitate collaboration among developers, testers, and other stakeholders involved in the software development lifecycle. Automated code reviews and test results can be easily shared and discussed, fostering knowledge sharing and ensuring alignment across teams.

Key Benefits

Enhanced code quality: By catching errors early and ensuring comprehensive testing, automated code review and testing significantly improves software quality and reliability.

Increased efficiency: Automation reduces the time and effort required for manual code reviews and testing, freeing developers to focus on more strategic and creative tasks.

Accelerated development: Faster feedback loops and continuous integration enable rapid iteration and delivery of software updates.

Improved collaboration: AI-powered tools facilitate communication and knowledge sharing among teams, leading to better alignment and collaboration.

Examples of Automated Code Review and Testing Tools

DeepCode: AI-powered code review platform that analyzes code for security vulnerabilities, bugs, and performance issues.

SonarQube: Open-source platform that leverages AI to analyze code quality, identify technical debt, and track code smells.

Selenium: Popular open-source framework for automating web browser testing.

Appium: Open-source framework for automating mobile app testing.

Conclusion

Automated code review and testing, powered by AI, are revolutionizing the quality assurance process in software development. By enhancing code quality, increasing efficiency, and facilitating collaboration, AI tools are empowering development teams to deliver high-quality software faster and with greater confidence.

Enhancing Code Quality Assurance

In the realm of software development, ensuring the quality and reliability of code is a continuous pursuit. Traditional code review and testing processes, often manual and time-consuming, can be prone to human error and oversight. AI is revolutionizing code quality assurance by introducing precision, automation, and a proactive approach to identifying and resolving issues, ultimately leading to more robust and resilient software.

AI-Powered Static Code Analysis

AI-driven static code analysis tools scan codebases for potential errors, bugs, security vulnerabilities, and performance bottlenecks. These tools go beyond simple syntax checks, leveraging machine learning algorithms to identify patterns, anomalies, and deviations from best practices that may indicate underlying problems. By automating the analysis of code, AI helps catch errors early in the development cycle, preventing them from cascading into larger issues and reducing the cost of rework.

Automated Test Case Generation and Execution

AI can significantly enhance testing efforts by automatically generating test cases based on code analysis, requirements, and user scenarios. This ensures comprehensive test coverage and reduces the risk of overlooking critical scenarios. AI-powered testing frameworks can then execute these test cases efficiently, identifying potential failures and regressions. This proactive approach to testing helps prevent bugs from reaching production and ensures software reliability.

Predictive Analytics and Early Issue Detection

AI can analyze historical data, code patterns, and user behavior to predict potential issues and vulnerabilities before they manifest in production. This predictive capability allows for proactive problem-solving and preventive measures, minimizing downtime and enhancing user satisfaction.

Continuous Integration and Continuous Delivery (CI/CD)

AI-powered CI/CD pipelines streamline the build, test, and deployment processes, enabling faster and more frequent software releases. By automating these processes, AI ensures that code changes are thoroughly tested and integrated before deployment, reducing the risk of integration issues and improving software stability.

Real-World Examples

DeepCode: This AI-powered code review platform utilizes machine learning to analyze code for potential security vulnerabilities, bugs, and performance issues, providing developers with actionable insights to improve code quality.

Amazon CodeGuru: This AI-powered tool offers intelligent recommendations for code reviews, identifying potential errors and suggesting improvements to enhance code quality and performance.

Testim.io: This AI-powered testing platform automates the creation, execution, and maintenance of test cases, ensuring comprehensive test coverage and faster feedback loops.

Conclusion

AI is transforming code quality assurance by introducing precision, automation, and a proactive approach to identifying and resolving issues. Through AI-powered tools and techniques, developers can catch errors early, ensure comprehensive testing, and prevent issues from reaching production, ultimately leading to higher-quality, more reliable software.

Embracing AI in code quality assurance is not just about improving software; it's about fostering a culture of continuous improvement and innovation. By leveraging AI's capabilities, development teams can focus on building exceptional software that meets the evolving needs of users and businesses while maintaining the highest standards of quality and reliability.

Identifying and Fixing Bugs Early

In the fast-paced world of software development, bugs are an unavoidable reality. These errors, ranging from minor glitches to critical vulnerabilities, can have significant consequences, impacting user experience, system stability, and even security. Traditionally, bug detection and resolution have relied heavily on manual testing and debugging, often leading to delays, increased costs, and frustrated users. However, AI is revolutionizing this landscape, empowering developers to identify and fix bugs early in the development cycle, resulting in more robust and reliable software.

AI-Powered Static Code Analysis

Static code analysis tools, enhanced with AI, meticulously scan codebases for potential errors, bugs, security vulnerabilities, and performance bottlenecks.

These tools go beyond simple syntax checks, leveraging machine learning algorithms to identify patterns, anomalies, and deviations from best practices that may indicate underlying problems. By automating the analysis of code, AI helps catch errors early in the development cycle, even before the code is executed.

This proactive approach prevents errors from propagating and causing costly issues later in the development process.

Automated Testing and Test Case Generation

AI-powered testing frameworks can automatically generate and execute test cases based on code analysis, requirements, and user scenarios. This ensures comprehensive test coverage and reduces the risk of overlooking critical scenarios that might trigger bugs.

Automated testing also allows for faster and more frequent testing, enabling continuous integration and continuous delivery (CI/CD) pipelines to operate seamlessly, providing immediate feedback on code changes and facilitating early bug detection.

Predictive Analytics and Early Issue Detection

AI's ability to analyze historical data, code patterns, and user behavior allows it to predict potential issues and vulnerabilities before they manifest in production. This predictive capability enables developers to take proactive measures and implement fixes before bugs impact users. By identifying potential problem areas early on, AI helps minimize downtime, enhance user satisfaction, and improve the overall quality of the software.

.

Accelerating the Testing Process

In the realm of software development, time-to-market is critical. The ability to test code quickly, thoroughly, and efficiently can make all the difference in meeting deadlines, delivering quality products, and staying ahead of the competition. AI is revolutionizing the testing process by automating tasks, optimizing test case generation, and providing intelligent insights, ultimately accelerating development cycles and ensuring robust software releases.

Automating Test Case Generation and Execution

AI-powered testing frameworks can automatically generate test cases based on code analysis, requirements, and user scenarios. This eliminates the need for manual test case creation, saving developers valuable time and reducing the risk of human errors. Additionally, AI can execute these test cases automatically, enabling faster and more frequent testing, thereby accelerating the feedback loop and facilitating continuous integration and continuous delivery (CI/CD) pipelines.

Intelligent Test Selection and Prioritization

AI can analyze code changes, historical test data, and code complexity to intelligently select and prioritize test cases. This ensures that the most critical and impactful tests are executed first, maximizing test coverage and reducing the time required to identify and address potential issues. By focusing on high-priority tests, AI helps optimize testing resources and accelerate the overall testing process.

Predictive Analytics and Early Issue Detection

AI can analyze historical data, code patterns, and user behavior to predict potential issues and vulnerabilities before they manifest in production. This predictive capability allows for proactive problem-solving and preventive measures, minimizing downtime and enhancing user satisfaction. By identifying potential bugs early, developers can address them before they impact users, further speeding up the testing process.

Self-Healing Test Scripts

AI-powered test scripts can adapt and evolve based on changes in the application's user interface or underlying code. This eliminates the need for manual updates to test scripts, saving time and ensuring that tests remain relevant and effective even as the software evolves.

Real-World Examples

Mabl: This AI-powered test automation platform uses machine learning to create, execute, and maintain automated tests, enabling faster and more reliable testing across different browsers and devices.

Testim.io: This AI-powered testing platform automates the creation, execution, and maintenance of test cases, ensuring comprehensive test coverage and faster feedback loops.

Functionize: This AI-powered testing platform uses natural language processing to create and execute tests, making test automation more accessible to non-technical users and accelerating the testing process.

Improving Collaboration and Communication

.In the world of software development, effective collaboration and communication are key to success. As projects grow in complexity and teams become more distributed, the need for seamless information sharing and coordination becomes even more critical. AI is emerging as a valuable tool in enhancing collaboration and communication within development teams, fostering a more cohesive and productive environment.

AI-Powered Code Reviews and Collaboration Platforms

AI-driven code review platforms leverage machine learning algorithms to analyze code changes, identify potential issues, and suggest improvements. This automates the review process, providing developers with instant feedback and fostering knowledge sharing. AI can also identify code patterns and suggest relevant experts within the team to review specific code sections, ensuring that the right people are involved in the review process.

Real-Time Communication and Collaboration Tools

AI-powered communication and collaboration tools facilitate seamless interaction among team members, regardless of their physical location. Chatbots and virtual assistants can answer common queries, provide project updates, and schedule meetings, freeing up valuable time for developers. AI-driven project management tools can track progress, allocate resources, and identify potential bottlenecks, ensuring that everyone is aligned and on track.

Knowledge Sharing and Documentation

AI can help capture and organize project knowledge, making it easily accessible to team members. AI-powered documentation tools can automatically generate documentation based on code analysis, comments, and discussions, ensuring that knowledge is preserved and shared effectively. Additionally, AI can assist in searching and retrieving relevant information from vast code repositories, enabling developers to quickly find answers and solutions.

Personalized Learning and Onboarding

AI can tailor learning experiences to individual needs and preferences, helping new team members onboard faster and more effectively. By analyzing learning patterns and providing personalized recommendations, AI can accelerate the learning curve and empower developers to contribute sooner.

Real-World Examples

GitHub Copilot: This AI-powered tool not only suggests code completions but also provides explanations and context, facilitating knowledge sharing and learning within teams.

Slack: This popular collaboration platform leverages AI to automate routine tasks, summarize conversations, and provide intelligent search capabilities, enhancing communication and information sharing.

Trello: This project management tool uses AI to automate task assignments, suggest deadlines, and identify potential risks, promoting collaboration and ensuring projects stay on track.

Chapter 5.

AI-Driven Debugging and Troubleshooting

In the intricate world of software development, debugging and troubleshooting are inevitable challenges that can consume valuable time and resources. AI is emerging as a game-changer in this domain, offering innovative solutions to streamline error identification, resolution, and prevention. By leveraging machine learning, pattern recognition, and predictive analytics, AI empowers developers to resolve issues swiftly and effectively, enhancing software reliability and user satisfaction.

Pinpointing Errors with Precision

AI-powered debugging tools analyze code, logs, and runtime data to identify the root causes of errors and exceptions. These tools go beyond simple stack traces, employing sophisticated algorithms to pinpoint the exact lines of code or configurations that are causing problems. This precision saves developers from tedious manual debugging and accelerates the resolution process.

Suggesting Fixes and Optimizations

AI doesn't just stop at identifying errors; it can also suggest fixes and optimizations based on best practices, historical data, and similar code patterns. This helps developers resolve issues faster and learn from previous solutions, fostering continuous improvement.

Predictive Analytics and Proactive Problem-Solving

AI can analyze patterns in code, logs, and system behavior to predict potential issues and vulnerabilities before they manifest in production. This proactive approach allows developers to address problems before they impact users, minimizing downtime and enhancing software reliability.

Automated Root Cause Analysis

AI can automate the process of root cause analysis, identifying the underlying causes of errors and exceptions. This saves developers significant time and effort, allowing them to focus on implementing fixes and preventing similar issues in the future.

Real-World Examples

Microsoft's Visual Studio IntelliCode: This AI-powered tool can identify potential errors in code and suggest fixes as developers write, improving code quality and reducing debugging time.

Amazon CodeGuru: This AI-powered service provides intelligent recommendations for code reviews, identifying potential issues and suggesting improvements to prevent errors.

Rookout: This dynamic observability platform leverages AI to collect and analyze debugging data in real-time, enabling developers to quickly identify and resolve issues in production environments.

AI-Driven Debugging in the Nigerian Context

In Nigeria's rapidly growing tech sector, AI-powered debugging and troubleshooting tools offer tremendous potential. These tools can help bridge the gap in expertise and resources, empowering smaller teams to build robust and reliable software. As Nigerian developers collaborate with international teams and contribute to global projects, AI-driven debugging tools can streamline communication and ensure seamless error resolution across diverse environments.

Pinpointing and Resolving Issues

In the intricate world of software development, debugging can be akin to finding a needle in a haystack. Traditional debugging methods often involve manually sifting through lines of code, logs, and stack traces, a process that can be time-consuming, frustrating, and error-prone. AI is revolutionizing this landscape by pinpointing errors with precision and providing intelligent insights that expedite issue resolution, saving developers valuable time and effort.

AI-Powered Error Identification

AI-driven debugging tools leverage machine learning algorithms and advanced analytics to analyze code, logs, and runtime data, identifying patterns and anomalies that may indicate underlying issues. These tools can automatically detect errors, exceptions, and performance bottlenecks, pinpointing the exact lines of code or configurations that are causing problems. This precision eliminates the guesswork and manual searching often associated with traditional debugging, enabling developers to focus on the core issue at hand.

Intelligent Root Cause Analysis

Beyond identifying errors, AI can delve deeper into the code and system behavior to perform root cause analysis. By analyzing the sequence of events leading up to an error, AI tools can trace the origin of the problem, identifying the underlying causes and potential dependencies. This comprehensive understanding of the root cause enables developers to implement targeted fixes, preventing similar issues from recurring in the future.

Real-Time Debugging and Monitoring

AI-powered debugging tools can operate in real-time, monitoring application behavior and identifying errors as they occur. This allows developers to address issues promptly, minimizing downtime and ensuring a seamless user experience. Real-time debugging also enables proactive problem-solving, allowing developers to identify and resolve issues before they escalate and impact users.

Contextual Insights and Recommendations

AI-driven debugging tools not only pinpoint errors but also provide contextual insights and recommendations to guide developers toward effective solutions. These tools can suggest fixes, offer code refactorings, or highlight best practices, empowering developers to resolve issues quickly and efficiently. This intelligent assistance accelerates the learning process and helps developers enhance their debugging skills.

Minimizing Downtime and Disruptions

In the realm of software development, downtime and disruptions can have severe consequences. From financial losses to damaged reputations and frustrated users, the impact of system outages can be far-reaching. AI is emerging as a valuable tool in minimizing downtime and disruptions, enabling proactive issue detection, faster resolution, and improved system stability.

Predictive Analytics and Early Warning Systems

AI can analyze patterns in system logs, performance metrics, and user behavior to predict potential issues and vulnerabilities before they cause disruptions. This predictive capability enables proactive problem-solving, allowing developers to address potential issues before they escalate and impact users. Early warning systems powered by AI can alert administrators and developers about potential issues, providing time for preventative measures and minimizing the risk of outages.

Real-Time Monitoring and Anomaly Detection

AI-powered monitoring tools can continuously observe system behavior, identifying anomalies and deviations from expected patterns. This allows for immediate detection of issues as they occur, enabling rapid response and minimizing the duration of outages. By detecting anomalies in real-time, AI tools can trigger alerts and even automate corrective actions, ensuring system stability and preventing disruptions.

Automated Root Cause Analysis and Resolution

When issues do occur, AI can help streamline the troubleshooting process. By analyzing logs, code, and system behavior, AI-powered tools can perform automated root cause analysis, identifying the underlying causes of errors and exceptions. This saves developers valuable time and effort, allowing them to focus on implementing fixes and restoring system functionality quickly.

Self-Healing Systems and Automated Recovery

AI can be used to build self-healing systems that can automatically detect and recover from failures. By monitoring critical components and identifying anomalies, AI can trigger automated recovery procedures, such as restarting services, rerouting traffic, or scaling resources, minimizing the impact of disruptions and ensuring system availability.

Real-World Examples

Dynatrace: This AI-powered monitoring and observability platform uses machine learning to detect anomalies and predict potential issues, allowing for proactive problem-solving and minimizing downtime.

Moogsoft: This AI-powered incident management platform utilizes machine learning to correlate alerts, identify root causes, and automate incident resolution, improving incident response times and reducing disruptions.

PagerDuty: This incident management platform leverages AI to automate incident routing and escalation, ensuring that the right people are notified and respond to issues promptly, minimizing downtime and impact on users.

Conclusion

AI is transforming the way developers and organizations approach system stability and reliability. By enabling proactive issue detection, faster resolution, and automated recovery, AI-powered tools are minimizing downtime and disruptions, leading to improved user experiences and business continuity.

As AI continues to evolve, we can expect even more sophisticated tools and techniques that will further enhance system stability and resilience, empowering businesses to thrive in an increasingly digital and interconnected world.

Enhancing System Reliability and Stability

In today's digital landscape, where software systems are the backbone of businesses and critical services, reliability and stability are paramount. Downtime, errors, and performance issues can lead to financial losses, damaged reputations, and frustrated users. AI is revolutionizing how developers approach system reliability and stability, offering proactive solutions to prevent issues, optimize performance, and ensure seamless user experiences.

Predictive Analytics and Proactive Issue Detection

AI algorithms analyze historical data, system logs, and performance metrics to identify patterns and anomalies that may indicate potential problems. By recognizing these patterns, AI can predict potential issues and vulnerabilities before they cause disruptions. This enables developers to take proactive measures, such as applying patches, optimizing configurations, or scaling resources, preventing downtime and ensuring system stability.

Anomaly Detection and Real-time Monitoring

AI-powered monitoring tools continuously observe system behavior, identifying deviations from expected patterns. This allows for immediate detection of anomalies and potential issues as they occur. By recognizing unusual behavior in real-time, AI tools can trigger alerts and even automate corrective actions, minimizing the impact of disruptions and maintaining system stability.

Automated Root Cause Analysis and Resolution

When issues do arise, AI can streamline the troubleshooting process. By analyzing logs, code, and system behavior, AI-powered tools can perform automated root cause analysis, identifying the underlying causes of errors and exceptions. This saves developers valuable time and effort, allowing them to focus on implementing targeted fixes and preventing similar issues in the future.

Self-Healing Systems and Automated Recovery

AI can be used to build self-healing systems that can automatically detect and recover from failures. By monitoring critical components and identifying anomalies, AI can trigger automated recovery procedures, such as restarting services, rerouting traffic, or scaling resources. This minimizes the impact of disruptions, ensuring system availability and maintaining uninterrupted services.

Performance Optimization and Resource Management

AI can analyze system performance data to identify bottlenecks and inefficiencies. By understanding resource utilization patterns and user behavior, AI can recommend optimizations, such as code refactorings, database tuning, or load balancing adjustments. This leads to improved system performance, reduced resource consumption, and enhanced user experiences.

Real-World Examples

Dynatrace: This AI-powered monitoring and observability platform uses machine learning to detect anomalies and predict potential issues, allowing for proactive problem-solving and minimizing downtime.

Moogsoft: This AI-powered incident management platform utilizes machine learning to correlate alerts, identify root causes, and automate incident resolution, improving incident response times and reducing disruptions.

AppDynamics: This application performance monitoring tool leverages AI to analyze application behavior, identify performance bottlenecks, and provide actionable insights for optimization.

Conclusion

AI is transforming the way developers approach system reliability and stability, offering proactive solutions to prevent issues, optimize performance, and ensure seamless user experiences. By embracing AI-powered tools and techniques, developers can build more robust and resilient software systems that meet the demands of today's digital landscape. As AI continues to evolve, we can expect even more sophisticated solutions that will further enhance system reliability and stability, empowering businesses and organizations to thrive in an increasingly interconnected world.

Empowering Proactive Problem-Solving

Traditionally, software development has often followed a reactive approach to problem-solving, where issues are addressed only after they occur, leading to downtime, disruptions, and frustrated users. AI is changing this paradigm by empowering developers with proactive problem-solving capabilities, enabling them to anticipate, prevent, and resolve issues before they impact users or system stability.

How AI Enables Proactive Problem-Solving:

Predictive Analytics and Early Warning Systems
AI algorithms analyze historical data, system logs, and performance metrics to identify patterns and anomalies that may indicate potential problems. By recognizing these patterns, AI can predict potential issues and vulnerabilities before they cause disruptions. This enables developers to take proactive measures such as:

Applying patches and updates preemptively
Optimizing configurations to prevent bottlenecks
Scaling resources to handle anticipated load increases
Implementing redundancy and failover mechanisms
Anomaly Detection and Real-time Monitoring
AI-powered monitoring tools continuously observe system behavior, identifying deviations from expected

patterns. This allows for immediate detection of anomalies and potential issues as they occur. By recognizing unusual behavior in real-time, AI tools can:

Trigger alerts to notify developers and operations teams
Automate corrective actions, such as restarting services or rerouting traffic
Provide real-time insights into system health and performance

Intelligent Recommendations and Insights

AI-powered tools can provide developers with intelligent recommendations and insights to help them proactively address potential issues. By analyzing code, logs, and system behavior, AI can suggest:

Code refactorings to improve maintainability and prevent future errors
Performance optimizations to enhance system responsiveness and efficiency
Security enhancements to protect against vulnerabilities
Knowledge Sharing and Collaboration

AI-powered platforms facilitate knowledge sharing and collaboration among developers, enabling them to learn from past experiences and avoid repeating mistakes. AI tools help teams:

Capture and organize project knowledge, making it easily accessible
Identify recurring issues and implement preventive measures
Connect developers with relevant experts to facilitate collaboration and accelerate problem-solving

Real-World Examples

Dynatrace: This AI-powered monitoring and observability platform uses machine learning to detect anomalies and predict potential issues, allowing for proactive problem-solving and minimizing downtime.

Logz.io: This AI-powered log analysis platform uses machine learning to identify patterns and anomalies in log data, providing developers with early warnings about potential issues.

Stack Overflow: This popular developer community platform leverages AI to suggest relevant questions and answers, helping developers find solutions to common problems and learn from others' experiences.

Conclusion

AI is transforming the way developers approach problem-solving, enabling a shift from reactive to proactive approaches. By predicting potential issues, identifying anomalies, and providing intelligent recommendations, AI empowers developers to prevent problems before they occur, leading to improved system reliability, enhanced user satisfaction, and accelerated development cycles. As AI continues to evolve, we can expect even more sophisticated tools and techniques that will further empower proactive problem-solving, driving innovation and progress in the software development landscape.

Empowering Proactive Problem-Solving

Traditionally, software development has often followed a reactive approach to problem-solving, where issues are addressed only after they occur, leading to downtime, disruptions, and frustrated users. AI is changing this paradigm by empowering developers with proactive problem-solving capabilities, enabling them to anticipate, prevent, and resolve issues before they impact users or system stability.

How AI Enables Proactive Problem-Solving:

Predictive Analytics and Early Warning Systems
AI algorithms analyze historical data, system logs, and performance metrics to identify patterns and anomalies that may indicate potential problems. By recognizing these patterns, AI can predict potential issues and

vulnerabilities before they cause disruptions. This enables developers to take proactive measures such as:

Applying patches and updates preemptively
Optimizing configurations to prevent bottlenecks
Scaling resources to handle anticipated load increases
Implementing redundancy and failover mechanisms

Anomaly Detection and Real-time Monitoring

AI-powered monitoring tools continuously observe system behavior, identifying deviations from expected patterns. This allows for immediate detection of anomalies and potential issues as they occur. By recognizing unusual behavior in real-time, AI tools can:

Trigger alerts to notify developers and operations teams
Automate corrective actions, such as restarting services or rerouting traffic
Provide real-time insights into system health and performance

Intelligent Recommendations and Insights

AI-powered tools can provide developers with intelligent recommendations and insights to help them proactively address potential issues. By analyzing code, logs, and system behavior, AI can suggest:

Code refactorings to improve maintainability and prevent future errors

Performance optimizations to enhance system responsiveness and efficiency

Security enhancements to protect against vulnerabilities

Knowledge Sharing and Collaboration

AI-powered platforms facilitate knowledge sharing and collaboration among developers, enabling them to learn from past experiences and avoid repeating mistakes. AI tools help teams:

Capture and organize project knowledge, making it easily accessible

Identify recurring issues and implement preventive measures

Connect developers with relevant experts to facilitate collaboration and accelerate problem-solving

Real-World Examples

Dynatrace: This AI-powered monitoring and observability platform uses machine learning to detect anomalies and predict potential issues, allowing for proactive problem-solving and minimizing downtime.
L
ogz.io: This AI-powered log analysis platform uses machine learning to identify patterns and anomalies in log data, providing developers with early warnings about potential issues.

Stack Overflow: This popular developer community platform leverages AI to suggest relevant questions and answers, helping developers find solutions to common problems and learn from others' experiences.

Conclusion

AI is transforming the way developers approach problem-solving, enabling a shift from reactive to proactive approaches. By predicting potential issues, identifying anomalies, and providing intelligent recommendations, AI empowers developers to prevent problems before they occur, leading to improved system reliability, enhanced user satisfaction, and accelerated development cycles. As AI continues to evolve, we can expect even more sophisticated tools and techniques that will further empower proactive problem-solving, driving innovation and progress in the software development landscape.

Chapter 6.

Machine Learning for Software Optimization

In the quest for building high-performing and user-centric software, Machine Learning (ML) emerges as a transformative ally. Beyond its role in automating tasks and assisting in coding, ML's data-driven insights and optimization capabilities are pushing the boundaries of software efficiency and user experience. By analyzing vast amounts of data generated during development and runtime, ML algorithms can identify performance bottlenecks, predict user behavior, and uncover hidden opportunities for improvement. This allows developers to fine-tune their code, optimize resource allocation, and create software that truly delights its users.

Analyzing and Improving Performance

.

In the pursuit of creating software that runs smoothly, efficiently, and delights users, performance optimization is a crucial aspect of development. Machine Learning (ML) offers a powerful arsenal of techniques to analyze, understand, and enhance software performance, transforming a traditionally laborious and time-consuming process into a data-driven and intelligent endeavor.

Unveiling Performance Bottlenecks

One of ML's most significant contributions to performance optimization is its ability to automatically identify bottlenecks in software systems. By analyzing vast amounts of runtime data, ML algorithms can detect patterns and anomalies that indicate areas where code execution is slowing down or resource utilization is inefficient.

These insights can reveal hidden performance issues that might otherwise go unnoticed, allowing developers to focus their optimization efforts on the most critical areas and achieve significant improvements.

Profiling and Resource Optimization

ML-powered profiling tools go beyond traditional profiling techniques by leveraging machine learning algorithms to provide deeper insights into code execution and resource usage. These tools can identify resource-intensive operations, memory leaks, and other performance bottlenecks, enabling developers to optimize code, improve algorithms, and fine-tune resource allocation for optimal performance.

Predictive Performance Modeling

ML can also be used to build predictive models of software performance, forecasting how changes in code, configuration, or usage patterns might impact system behavior. These models can help developers anticipate potential performance issues and make informed decisions about optimization strategies before deploying changes to production.

Automated Performance Testing

AI-powered performance testing tools can automate the execution of performance tests, simulating various user loads and scenarios. These tools can collect and analyze performance data in real-time, identifying performance regressions and helping developers quickly identify and address performance issues.

Continuous Performance Improvement

ML enables a culture of continuous performance improvement by continuously monitoring system behavior and providing ongoing feedback to developers. This allows for proactive optimization and ensures that software remains performant even as usage patterns and system loads evolve.

Real-world examples:

Google's PerfKit Explorer: This AI-powered tool analyzes performance data from Chrome browsers, helping developers identify and fix performance bottlenecks in web applications.

AppDynamics: This application performance monitoring tool leverages machine learning to detect anomalies and predict potential performance issues, allowing for proactive optimization.

Datadog: This cloud monitoring platform uses machine learning to analyze logs, metrics, and traces, helping developers identify performance issues and optimize their infrastructure.

Conclusion:

Machine learning is revolutionizing the way developers analyze and improve software performance. By providing data-driven insights, automating testing, and enabling predictive modeling, ML empowers developers to identify and address performance bottlenecks, optimize resource allocation, and create software that is both efficient and responsive. As ML continues to evolve, we can expect even more sophisticated tools and techniques that will further enhance software performance and deliver exceptional user experiences.

Identifying and Addressing Bottlenecks

In the pursuit of optimal software performance, identifying and addressing bottlenecks is crucial. Traditionally, this has been a time-consuming and complex process, requiring manual profiling, code analysis, and extensive testing. AI is revolutionizing this landscape by providing developers with powerful tools and techniques to pinpoint bottlenecks efficiently and implement targeted optimizations, ensuring smooth and responsive software experiences.

AI-Powered Bottleneck Identification

AI-driven performance analysis tools leverage machine learning algorithms to analyze system logs, performance metrics, and code execution traces, identifying areas where the software is experiencing slowdowns or inefficiencies. These tools can automatically detect resource-intensive operations, memory leaks, and other performance bottlenecks, highlighting areas that require optimization.

Real-Time Monitoring and Anomaly Detection

AI-powered monitoring tools continuously observe system behavior, identifying deviations from expected patterns. This allows for immediate detection of performance anomalies and potential bottlenecks as they occur. By recognizing unusual behavior in real-time, AI tools can trigger alerts and even automate corrective actions, minimizing the impact of bottlenecks and ensuring system responsiveness.

Root Cause Analysis and Targeted Optimization

AI not only identifies bottlenecks but also assists in root cause analysis, determining the underlying causes of performance issues. This enables developers to implement targeted optimizations, such as code refactorings, database tuning, or algorithm improvements, addressing the root cause and preventing similar bottlenecks from recurring.

Predictive Analytics and Capacity Planning

AI can analyze historical data and usage patterns to predict future performance trends and resource requirements. This enables proactive capacity planning, ensuring that the system has sufficient resources to handle anticipated loads and prevent bottlenecks from occurring due to resource constraints.

Real-World Examples

New Relic: This application performance monitoring tool leverages AI to analyze application behavior, identify performance bottlenecks, and provide actionable insights for optimization.
Instana: This AI-powered observability platform automatically discovers and maps application dependencies, identifying bottlenecks and enabling faster troubleshooting and optimization.

Elastic APM: This application performance monitoring tool utilizes machine learning to detect anomalies and identify root causes of performance issues, facilitating efficient optimization.

Conclusion

AI is transforming the way developers identify and address bottlenecks in software systems. By providing intelligent insights, real-time monitoring, and proactive solutions, AI-powered tools empower developers to optimize performance, ensure system stability, and deliver exceptional user experiences.

As AI continues to evolve, we can expect even more sophisticated tools and techniques that will further enhance bottleneck identification and resolution, enabling developers to build high-performing software that meets the demands of today's digital landscape.

Enhancing User Experience and Satisfaction

In today's competitive landscape, user experience (UX) and satisfaction are critical factors in the success of any software product. Users expect software to be not only functional but also intuitive, responsive, and personalized to their needs. AI is playing a transformative role in enhancing UX and satisfaction, enabling developers to create software that delights users and keeps them engaged.

Personalized Recommendations and Content

AI algorithms can analyze user behavior, preferences, and historical data to provide personalized recommendations and content. This can range from suggesting relevant products or services to tailoring news feeds and social media content. By delivering personalized experiences, AI helps users discover content that resonates with them, increasing engagement and satisfaction.

Intelligent Chatbots and Virtual Assistants

AI-powered chatbots and virtual assistants provide instant support and guidance to users, answering questions, resolving issues, and guiding them through complex tasks. These intelligent agents can understand natural language queries, offer personalized assistance, and even proactively anticipate user needs, creating a seamless and supportive user experience.

Predictive Analytics and Proactive Support

AI can analyze user behavior and system data to predict potential issues and proactively offer solutions. This can include identifying and addressing potential bugs, suggesting optimizations, or providing personalized tips and tutorials. By anticipating user needs and proactively offering assistance, AI can prevent frustration and enhance user satisfaction.

Accessibility and Inclusivity

AI can be used to make software more accessible and inclusive for users with disabilities. For example, AI-powered tools can generate captions for videos, provide screen reader support, and even interpret sign language. By incorporating AI-driven accessibility features, developers can create software that is welcoming and usable for everyone.

User Behavior Analysis and Continuous Improvement

AI can analyze user behavior and feedback to identify areas for improvement in the software. By understanding how users interact with the software, AI can help developers identify pain points, optimize workflows, and prioritize features that enhance the user experience. This data-driven approach to improvement ensures that the software evolves to meet the changing needs and expectations of users.

Real-World Examples

Netflix: This popular streaming service uses AI to provide personalized recommendations to users based on their viewing history and preferences.

Amazon Alexa: This AI-powered virtual assistant can answer questions, control smart home devices, and provide personalized recommendations.

Grammarly: This AI-powered writing assistant helps users improve their writing by suggesting grammar corrections, style improvements, and even tone adjustments.

Conclusion

AI is revolutionizing the way developers approach user experience and satisfaction, enabling them to create software that is not only functional but also intuitive, personalized, and delightful. By leveraging AI's capabilities in personalization, intelligent assistance, predictive analytics, accessibility, and continuous improvement, developers can build software that truly resonates with users and fosters long-term engagement.

As AI continues to evolve, we can expect even more sophisticated and impactful solutions that will further enhance user experience and satisfaction, shaping the future of software design and interaction.

Driving Continuous Improvement

In the dynamic landscape of software development, the pursuit of perfection is an ongoing journey. The ability to iterate, learn, and adapt is crucial for staying ahead of the curve and delivering exceptional software solutions that evolve with user needs and technological advancements. AI is proving to be a catalyst for driving continuous improvement in the software development lifecycle, enabling data-driven insights, automated feedback loops, and intelligent optimization that propel software quality, performance, and user satisfaction to new heights.

Data-Driven Insights and Feedback

AI empowers developers with a wealth of data-driven insights into their software's performance, user behavior, and potential areas for improvement. By analyzing vast amounts of data generated during development, testing, and real-world usage, AI algorithms can identify patterns, trends, and anomalies that shed light on areas where the software can be enhanced. This data-driven feedback enables developers to make informed decisions, prioritize enhancements, and continuously refine their code to meet evolving needs.

Automated Feedback Loops and Continuous Testing

AI enables the creation of automated feedback loops that seamlessly integrate into the development process. Continuous integration and continuous delivery (CI/CD) pipelines, powered by AI, automate the build, test, and deployment process, providing developers with immediate feedback on code changes. This accelerates the identification and resolution of issues, ensuring that software is always in a releasable state and minimizing the risk of regressions.

Intelligent Optimization and Adaptation

AI algorithms can learn from user interactions, system behavior, and performance data to suggest optimizations and adaptations. This can include code refactorings, algorithm improvements, and even dynamic adjustments to user interfaces based on individual preferences and usage patterns. By continuously learning and adapting, AI helps developers optimize software performance, enhance user experiences, and stay ahead of evolving requirements.

Proactive Issue Detection and Prevention

AI's predictive capabilities empower developers to anticipate and prevent potential issues before they impact users. By analyzing historical data and patterns, AI can identify potential vulnerabilities, performance bottlenecks, and security risks. This proactive approach allows developers to address issues early in the development cycle, minimizing the risk of disruptions and ensuring a more stable and reliable software experience.

Conclusion

AI is playing a pivotal role in driving continuous improvement in software development. By providing data-driven insights, automating feedback loops, and enabling intelligent optimization, AI empowers developers to create software that is not only functional and reliable but also constantly evolving and improving. Embracing AI's potential for continuous improvement is essential for any development team that aspires to build exceptional software and stay ahead in today's dynamic and competitive landscape.

Chapter 7.

Advanced AI Techniques in Software Development

As the capabilities of artificial intelligence continue to evolve, so too does its potential to revolutionize software development. Beyond the basic automation and optimization tasks, advanced AI techniques are now being leveraged to tackle more complex challenges and innovate in ways that were previously unimaginable. These techniques—ranging from Natural Language Processing (NLP) and Computer Vision to Deep Learning and Reinforcement Learning—are empowering developers to create smarter, more intuitive, and highly efficient software systems.

In this chapter, we will explore how these advanced AI techniques are being applied within the realm of software development. We'll dive into the intricacies of NLP and its ability to interpret and generate human language, enabling more natural interactions between developers and machines. We'll examine how Computer

Vision is transforming user interfaces and improving accessibility by allowing software to perceive and process visual information. The power of Deep Learning will be highlighted through its applications in predictive analytics, pattern recognition, and complex problem-solving. Finally, we'll explore Reinforcement Learning, a technique that allows software to learn and adapt through trial and error, paving the way for self-improving systems.

By understanding and harnessing these advanced AI techniques, developers can push the boundaries of what software can achieve, creating applications that are not only more intelligent but also more responsive to the needs of their users. This chapter will provide you with the knowledge and insights needed to integrate these cutting-edge technologies into your development process, ensuring that your software solutions remain at the forefront of innovation.

Natural Language Processing (NLP)

Natural Language Processing (NLP) stands at the intersection of artificial intelligence and linguistics, enabling machines to understand, interpret, and generate human language. As a branch of AI, NLP is designed to bridge the gap between human communication and computer understanding, making it possible for machines to process and respond to text and speech in a way that is both meaningful and contextually relevant.

In the context of software development, NLP has opened up new possibilities for creating more intuitive and user-friendly applications. By incorporating NLP, developers can build systems that understand user commands, process complex queries, and even generate human-like text. This capability is particularly powerful in areas such as chatbots, voice-activated assistants, and automated content generation, where natural language interactions are crucial.

One of the key applications of NLP in software development is in code comprehension and documentation. With the ability to parse and analyze programming languages alongside human languages, NLP tools can assist developers in understanding codebases, automating documentation, and even translating code from one language to another. This not only enhances productivity but also makes the development process more accessible to those who may not be experts in a particular programming language.

NLP also plays a significant role in improving the developer experience through intelligent code completion and error detection. By understanding the context of the code being written, NLP-powered tools can suggest relevant code snippets, detect potential errors, and offer corrections that are contextually appropriate. This reduces the cognitive load on developers and helps maintain code quality by preventing common mistakes.

Furthermore, NLP is crucial in creating software that interacts with users in natural and meaningful ways. For instance, in customer service applications, NLP-driven chatbots can handle complex queries by understanding the nuances of human language, offering accurate and helpful responses. In content management systems, NLP can automate tasks such as content categorization, sentiment analysis, and even the generation of summaries or reports.

The power of NLP extends beyond traditional software applications into the realm of data analysis. By applying NLP techniques to large datasets, developers can extract valuable insights from unstructured data, such as customer reviews, social media posts, and support tickets. This capability allows businesses to gain a deeper understanding of their customers and make data-driven decisions.

As NLP technology continues to advance, its potential applications in software development are expanding. From enhancing user interfaces to automating complex tasks, NLP is transforming how we interact with software and how software interacts with us. By integrating NLP into their projects, developers can create more intelligent, responsive, and human-centric applications that not only meet user needs but also anticipate them.

In summary, Natural Language Processing is a powerful tool in the software developer's arsenal, enabling the creation of more sophisticated and user-friendly applications. As AI continues to evolve, the role of NLP in software development will only grow, driving innovation and setting new standards for what software can achieve.

Computer Vision

Computer Vision, a field of artificial intelligence that enables machines to interpret and understand visual information from the world, is reshaping the landscape of software development. By equipping computers with the ability to process and analyze images and videos, Computer Vision is empowering developers to create applications that can "see" and respond to their environment, much like humans do. This technology is integral to a wide range of applications, from autonomous vehicles and facial recognition systems to augmented reality and healthcare diagnostics.

In the realm of software development, Computer Vision is being leveraged to enhance user interfaces, improve accessibility, and create more interactive and engaging experiences. For example, applications that incorporate facial recognition can offer personalized user experiences, such as unlocking devices or tailoring content recommendations based on user identity. In e-commerce, Computer Vision is enabling virtual try-on features, where users can see how clothes or accessories would look on them before making a purchase, thereby enhancing the online shopping experience.

One of the most impactful applications of Computer Vision in software development is in the field of augmented reality (AR). By using real-time image processing, Computer Vision allows AR applications to overlay digital content onto the real world, creating immersive experiences for users. This technology is widely used in gaming, retail, education, and even industrial design, where it can help visualize products in a real-world context before they are manufactured.

In healthcare, Computer Vision is playing a transformative role by assisting in diagnostics and treatment planning. For instance, software powered by Computer Vision can analyze medical images—such as X-rays, MRIs, and CT scans—to detect anomalies and assist doctors in diagnosing conditions more accurately and quickly. This not only enhances the accuracy of diagnoses but also helps in early detection of diseases, improving patient outcomes.

Beyond enhancing user experiences and healthcare, Computer Vision is also being used in software development to improve security and safety. Surveillance systems powered by Computer Vision can detect unusual activities or unauthorized access in real-time, providing businesses and governments with advanced tools for security monitoring. In autonomous vehicles, Computer Vision is crucial for enabling cars to navigate roads, recognize traffic signals, and avoid obstacles, thereby ensuring safe and efficient transportation.

For developers, integrating Computer Vision into software projects involves leveraging various algorithms and models that can process and analyze visual data. Techniques such as object detection, image segmentation, and pattern recognition are central to making sense of visual inputs. With the rise of powerful libraries and frameworks—such as OpenCV, TensorFlow, and PyTorch—developers can now more easily implement Computer Vision functionalities in their applications, even without deep expertise in the underlying AI techniques.

Another significant area where Computer Vision is making an impact is in accessibility. By enabling software to recognize and describe visual content, Computer Vision can assist users with visual impairments in navigating digital and physical environments. For instance, apps can read text aloud from images or provide audio descriptions of scenes captured by a camera, making technology more inclusive and accessible to all users.

As the capabilities of Computer Vision continue to expand, its applications in software development are becoming more diverse and powerful. Whether it's enhancing user interfaces, enabling new forms of interaction, or improving safety and accessibility, Computer Vision is at the forefront of innovation in software development. By incorporating this technology into their projects, developers can create more intelligent, responsive, and human-centric applications that not only meet but exceed user expectations.

In conclusion, Computer Vision is a rapidly evolving field that is transforming software development across multiple domains. As more developers explore its potential, we can expect to see even more innovative and impactful applications that leverage the power of visual understanding to solve real-world problems and create richer user experiences.

Deep Learning

Deep Learning, a subset of machine learning based on artificial neural networks, has become one of the most transformative technologies in software development. By mimicking the structure and function of the human brain, deep learning models are capable of learning from large amounts of data, identifying patterns, and making decisions with unprecedented accuracy. This ability to "learn" from data makes deep learning particularly powerful for complex tasks that are challenging for traditional algorithms, such as image recognition, natural language processing, and predictive analytics.

In software development, deep learning is opening new frontiers by enabling the creation of applications that can understand, predict, and adapt in ways that were once thought impossible. One of the most prominent applications of deep learning is in the field of computer vision, where it powers image and video recognition systems. For example, deep learning models are used in autonomous vehicles to interpret and react to visual information from the environment, allowing cars to navigate roads safely and efficiently. Similarly, in healthcare, deep learning is used to analyze medical images, helping doctors detect diseases like cancer with higher accuracy.

Natural Language Processing (NLP) is another area where deep learning is making significant strides. By utilizing deep learning techniques, NLP models can understand and generate human language with remarkable precision. This has led to the development of advanced chatbots, virtual assistants, and language translation services that can engage in more natural and meaningful conversations with users. Deep learning has also made it possible to build models that can summarize text, answer questions, and even generate creative content like poetry or code, pushing the boundaries of what software can achieve in terms of language understanding.

Deep learning is also revolutionizing predictive analytics and data-driven decision-making in software development. By analyzing vast datasets, deep learning models can uncover hidden patterns and correlations that are not immediately obvious to human analysts. This capability is being used in various industries to predict customer behavior, optimize supply chains, and improve financial forecasting. For instance, e-commerce platforms use deep learning to personalize product recommendations, increasing user engagement and sales. In finance, deep learning models are used to detect fraudulent transactions in real-time, safeguarding users and institutions from financial loss.

The impact of deep learning extends to other advanced AI techniques such as reinforcement learning, where it is used to train models that can learn and adapt through trial and error. This approach is particularly useful in scenarios where the optimal solution is not known in advance, such as in game development or robotics. By combining deep learning with reinforcement learning, developers can create intelligent systems that improve their performance over time, making decisions that are increasingly effective based on the outcomes of previous actions.

In software development, implementing deep learning involves working with large datasets and powerful computational resources. The availability of deep learning frameworks like TensorFlow, PyTorch, and Keras has made it easier for developers to build and deploy deep learning models, even without extensive expertise in AI. These frameworks provide pre-built models, libraries, and tools that simplify the process of training and fine-tuning deep learning models, allowing developers to focus on solving specific problems rather than dealing with the complexities of neural network architecture.

However, while deep learning offers immense potential, it also presents certain challenges. Training deep learning models often requires large amounts of labeled data and substantial computational power, which can be resource-intensive. Additionally, deep learning models can sometimes behave as "black boxes," making it difficult to interpret how they arrive at certain decisions. This lack of transparency can be a concern in critical applications, such as healthcare or finance, where understanding the reasoning behind a decision is crucial. Developers must also be mindful of ethical considerations, such as the potential for bias in deep learning models, which can arise from biased training data.

Despite these challenges, the benefits of deep learning in software development are undeniable. Its ability to process and analyze complex data, coupled with its adaptability and scalability, makes it a powerful tool for innovation. As deep learning technology continues to evolve, it will enable the creation of more intelligent, adaptive, and responsive software systems that can tackle a wide range of complex tasks with greater efficiency and accuracy.

In summary, deep learning is a cornerstone of modern AI that is driving significant advancements in software development. By harnessing the power of deep neural networks, developers can create applications that not only perform tasks more accurately but also learn and improve over time. As deep learning continues to mature, its influence on the future of software development will only grow, leading to more sophisticated and intelligent solutions that push the boundaries of what technology can achieve.

Reinforcement Learning

Reinforcement Learning (RL) is a dynamic and powerful branch of artificial intelligence that focuses on training algorithms through interaction with an environment. Unlike traditional supervised learning, where models learn from a set of labeled data, reinforcement learning involves an agent learning to make decisions by taking actions in an environment to maximize cumulative rewards over time. This trial-and-error approach allows the agent to learn optimal strategies or policies that can adapt to changing conditions and complex scenarios.

In the context of software development, reinforcement learning is particularly valuable for applications that require adaptive decision-making and continuous improvement. One of the most well-known applications of RL is in game development, where it has been used to create AI agents capable of playing games at superhuman levels. For example, RL algorithms have been employed to develop AI that can master complex games like Go, Chess, and video games such as StarCraft II, often surpassing human performance by learning and refining strategies through countless simulations and gameplay.

Beyond gaming, reinforcement learning is increasingly being applied to real-world problems in robotics, autonomous systems, and resource management. In robotics, RL is used to train robots to perform tasks such as walking, grasping objects, and navigating complex environments. By continuously interacting with their surroundings and receiving feedback, these robots can learn to perform tasks more efficiently and effectively over time. This capability is essential for developing robots that can adapt to new and unpredictable environments, making RL a critical component in the advancement of autonomous machines.

In autonomous vehicles, reinforcement learning is used to teach cars how to drive by learning from millions of simulated and real-world driving experiences. Through this process, the vehicle learns to navigate roads, avoid obstacles, and make decisions that ensure safety and efficiency. RL helps these vehicles adapt to different driving conditions and environments, improving their performance as they accumulate more data from their interactions with the real world.

Reinforcement learning is also being applied in resource management and optimization, where it can be used to optimize complex systems such as supply chains, energy grids, and financial portfolios. In these scenarios, RL agents learn to make decisions that balance competing objectives, such as minimizing costs while maximizing efficiency or profits. For instance, in supply chain management, RL can optimize inventory levels, production schedules, and distribution routes by learning from historical data and real-time feedback, leading to more efficient and cost-effective operations.

Another exciting application of reinforcement learning in software development is in personalized recommendations and adaptive systems. For example, streaming services and e-commerce platforms can use RL to dynamically adjust recommendations based on user behavior, improving user engagement and satisfaction.

By continuously learning from user interactions, RL models can refine their recommendations, providing increasingly relevant and personalized content or product suggestions over time.

The integration of reinforcement learning into software development does come with challenges. RL models typically require a significant amount of training data and computational resources, especially when dealing with complex environments. The exploration-exploitation trade-off is another critical aspect of RL; the agent must balance exploring new actions to discover their potential benefits with exploiting known actions that yield high rewards. Striking the right balance is crucial for achieving optimal performance, but it can be difficult to manage, especially in dynamic and uncertain environments.

Moreover, ensuring the safety and stability of RL-driven systems is essential, particularly in high-stakes applications like autonomous vehicles or healthcare. Developers must carefully design reward functions and constraints to prevent unintended behavior that could lead to negative consequences. Additionally, interpretability and transparency of RL models are important considerations, as these models can sometimes be seen as "black boxes" due to the complexity of their decision-making processes.

Despite these challenges, the potential of reinforcement learning in software development is immense. Its ability to enable systems to learn and adapt in real-time makes it a powerful tool for creating more intelligent, autonomous, and efficient applications. As reinforcement learning techniques continue to evolve, they will unlock new possibilities for innovation across a wide range of industries.

In summary, reinforcement learning is a cutting-edge AI technique that empowers software systems to learn from their interactions with the environment and make decisions that maximize long-term rewards. Its applications in gaming, robotics, autonomous systems, and beyond are transforming the way we approach complex problem-solving and optimization. As developers continue to harness the power of reinforcement learning, we can expect to see more adaptive, intelligent, and autonomous software systems that push the boundaries of what technology can achieve.

Chapter 8.

The Future of AI in Software Development

As we stand on the cusp of a new era in technology, artificial intelligence is poised to fundamentally reshape the landscape of software development. The integration of AI into development processes has already led to remarkable innovations, enhancing productivity, automating complex tasks, and creating more intelligent and responsive applications. However, the potential of AI in software development is far from fully realized. The future promises even more transformative advancements as AI continues to evolve, bringing forth new tools, techniques, and possibilities that will redefine how software is designed, built, and maintained.

In this chapter, we will explore the exciting prospects for AI in the world of software development. We'll examine the potential for groundbreaking innovation and growth as AI becomes more deeply embedded in every aspect of development, from code generation and debugging to testing and deployment. The chapter will also delve into the ethical considerations that arise with the increasing reliance on AI, emphasizing the importance of responsible development practices and the need to address biases and transparency in AI-driven systems.

Furthermore, as AI technology rapidly advances, there is an urgent need for continuous learning and adaptation within the development community. Developers must stay ahead of the curve, not only mastering new AI tools but also understanding their implications and potential impacts. This chapter will highlight the importance of cultivating a mindset of lifelong learning and flexibility to thrive in an AI-powered future.

Ultimately, the future of AI in software development is one of immense opportunity. By embracing AI and its potential, developers can unlock new levels of efficiency, creativity, and innovation, leading to software solutions that are not only more powerful but also more attuned to the needs of users. As we look forward, this chapter will provide insights into how AI will continue to shape the future of software development and what steps developers can take to prepare for and leverage the full potential of this transformative technology.

The Potential for Innovation and Growth

The integration of artificial intelligence into software development holds vast potential for driving innovation and fostering growth across industries. As AI technologies continue to evolve, they are set to revolutionize the way software is conceived, developed, and deployed, unlocking new opportunities for developers and businesses alike. The potential for innovation and growth in this space is immense, driven by AI's ability to automate complex tasks, enhance decision-making processes, and create more intelligent and adaptive applications.

One of the most significant areas where AI is poised to drive innovation is in automating routine and repetitive tasks within the software development lifecycle. Traditionally, developers spend considerable time on tasks such as writing boilerplate code, debugging, testing, and code reviews. AI-powered tools can automate these processes, allowing developers to focus on more creative and strategic aspects of development. For example, AI-driven code generators can produce functional code based on high-level descriptions, significantly reducing the time required to develop software. This not only accelerates development timelines but also lowers costs, making it easier for startups and small businesses to bring new products to market.

AI is also enabling the creation of more sophisticated and intelligent software applications that can learn, adapt, and evolve over time. Machine learning models, for instance, can be integrated into software to provide predictive analytics, personalized recommendations, and dynamic content generation. These capabilities allow businesses to offer more tailored and responsive experiences to users, enhancing customer satisfaction and engagement. In sectors such as healthcare, finance, and retail, AI-driven applications are already making a significant impact by improving decision-making, optimizing operations, and delivering personalized services.

Furthermore, AI is driving innovation in the way software interacts with users. Natural Language Processing (NLP) and computer vision technologies are being used to create more intuitive and accessible user interfaces. Voice-activated assistants, chatbots, and augmented reality applications are just a few examples of how AI is transforming user interactions. These innovations are not only enhancing user experiences but also opening up new possibilities for how software can be used in everyday life, from hands-free control of devices to real-time language translation and immersive digital environments.

The growth potential of AI in software development is also evident in its ability to scale and optimize operations. AI-powered tools can analyze vast amounts of data to identify patterns, optimize resource allocation, and predict future trends. This capability is particularly valuable in industries that rely on large-scale data processing, such as finance, logistics, and manufacturing. By leveraging AI, businesses can achieve greater efficiency, reduce waste, and make more informed decisions, driving growth and competitive advantage.

Moreover, the advent of AI in software development is democratizing access to advanced technology. Low-code and no-code platforms, powered by AI, are enabling individuals with little to no programming experience to create sophisticated applications. This democratization is fostering a new wave of innovation as more people, including non-developers, can participate in the software development process. As a result, we are likely to see an explosion of new ideas and solutions emerging from diverse perspectives and industries, further fueling growth and innovation.

However, the potential for innovation and growth through AI in software development is not without its challenges. As AI systems become more complex, there is a growing need for transparency, accountability, and ethical considerations in their design and deployment. Developers must navigate issues such as bias in AI models, data privacy, and the implications of automating decision-making processes. Addressing these challenges will be critical to ensuring that the growth driven by AI is sustainable and beneficial to society as a whole.

In conclusion, the potential for innovation and growth in software development through AI is vast and far-reaching. As AI technologies continue to advance, they will transform how software is developed, how businesses operate, and how users interact with technology. By embracing AI, developers and businesses can unlock new opportunities for creativity, efficiency, and scalability, driving the next wave of innovation in the digital age. The future of software development, powered by AI, promises to be one of continuous growth, where the boundaries of what is possible are constantly being redefined.

The Importance of Ethical Considerations

As artificial intelligence (AI) becomes increasingly integral to software development, the importance of ethical considerations cannot be overstated. While AI offers tremendous potential for innovation, efficiency, and growth, it also presents significant challenges and risks that must be carefully managed. Ensuring that AI-driven software is developed and deployed responsibly is crucial for maintaining trust, fairness, and accountability in an AI-powered future.

One of the primary ethical concerns in AI development is the potential for bias in AI models. AI systems learn from data, and if the training data reflects societal biases—such as those related to race, gender, or socioeconomic status—those biases can be perpetuated and even amplified by AI-driven applications. For instance, biased AI models in hiring software could unfairly disadvantage certain groups, while biased algorithms in criminal justice systems could lead to unjust outcomes. Developers must take proactive steps to identify, mitigate, and prevent bias in AI models by ensuring diverse and representative datasets, as well as by implementing fairness-aware algorithms.

Transparency and explainability are also critical ethical considerations in AI development. Many AI models, particularly deep learning systems, operate as "black boxes," making decisions in ways that are not easily understood by humans. This lack of transparency can be problematic, especially in high-stakes applications like healthcare, finance, or law enforcement, where understanding the reasoning behind an AI's decision is essential. Developers need to prioritize creating AI systems that are not only accurate but also interpretable, providing clear explanations for how decisions are made. This transparency is key to building trust with users and stakeholders, who need confidence that AI-driven decisions are made fairly and logically.

Data privacy is another major ethical concern in the age of AI. AI systems often rely on vast amounts of data to function effectively, raising questions about how that data is collected, stored, and used. With increasing public awareness of privacy issues, developers must ensure that AI-driven software adheres to strict data protection standards, such as the General Data Protection Regulation (GDPR) in Europe. This involves implementing robust data anonymization techniques, securing user consent for data collection, and providing users with control over their personal information. By safeguarding data privacy, developers can prevent misuse of data and protect users from potential harm.

The ethical implications of automating decision-making processes also warrant careful consideration. As AI takes on more roles traditionally performed by humans, there is a risk that critical decisions—such as those related to healthcare, legal judgments, or financial investments—could be made without adequate human oversight. While AI can enhance decision-making by providing data-driven insights, it is essential to maintain a balance where human judgment remains central, particularly in contexts that involve moral or ethical dilemmas. Developers should design AI systems that support and augment human decision-making, rather than replacing it entirely, ensuring that there is always a human in the loop when necessary.

In addition to these concerns, the broader societal impact of AI-driven software must be considered. The automation of tasks through AI has the potential to disrupt labor markets, leading to job displacement in certain sectors. While AI can create new opportunities and industries, it is important for developers and businesses to consider the social implications of their innovations. This includes investing in retraining programs, supporting workforce transitions, and contributing to policies that promote inclusive growth.

Lastly, developers must be vigilant about the potential misuse of AI technologies. As AI becomes more powerful, there is an increased risk that it could be used for harmful purposes, such as creating deepfakes, spreading misinformation, or enabling surveillance. Ethical AI development involves not only creating technology that benefits society but also anticipating and mitigating potential risks and abuses. Developers have a responsibility to establish guidelines and safeguards that prevent the malicious use of AI and to collaborate with policymakers, ethicists, and the broader community to ensure that AI is used for the greater good.

In conclusion, ethical considerations are paramount in the development and deployment of AI-driven software. As AI continues to shape the future of software development, developers must prioritize fairness, transparency, privacy, and accountability in their work. By addressing these ethical challenges, developers can help ensure that AI contributes positively to society, fostering innovation and growth while safeguarding the rights and well-being of individuals and communities. The ethical development of AI is not just a technical challenge—it is a moral imperative that will define the legacy of AI in the digital age.

The Need for Continuous Learning and Adaptation

In the rapidly evolving landscape of software development, continuous learning and adaptation have become essential for staying ahead of the curve. As artificial intelligence (AI) and other advanced technologies reshape the industry, developers, engineers, and organizations must embrace a mindset of ongoing education and flexibility to remain competitive and innovative.

The pace of technological advancement in AI is unprecedented. New algorithms, tools, frameworks, and best practices are constantly emerging, each offering new possibilities for enhancing software development processes. For developers, this means that the skills and knowledge that were relevant just a few years ago may quickly become outdated. To thrive in this dynamic environment, developers must commit to continuous learning, regularly updating their skill sets and staying informed about the latest trends and breakthroughs in AI.

One of the key areas where continuous learning is vital is in understanding and leveraging new AI tools and frameworks. As AI becomes more integrated into software development, a wide range of specialized tools are being developed to automate tasks, optimize workflows, and enhance code quality. From AI-driven code completion tools to automated testing frameworks, these technologies are revolutionizing the way software is built. However, effectively utilizing these tools requires developers to stay up-to-date with the latest advancements and to develop a deep understanding of how these tools can be applied to their specific projects. This involves not only learning how to use the tools but also understanding their underlying principles and limitations.

Beyond technical skills, continuous learning also encompasses staying informed about the broader implications of AI in software development. This includes understanding the ethical considerations, regulatory requirements, and societal impacts of AI-driven software. As AI increasingly influences decision-making processes and interacts with users in more sophisticated ways, developers need to be aware of the potential biases, privacy concerns, and ethical dilemmas that may arise. Continuous learning in this context means not only keeping up with technical developments but also engaging with ongoing debates and discussions about the responsible use of AI.

Adaptation is another crucial component of thriving in the AI-driven future of software development. As AI technologies evolve, they often bring about changes in workflows, team structures, and business models. Developers and organizations must be willing to adapt to these changes, rethinking traditional approaches to software development and embracing new methodologies that are better suited to the capabilities of AI. For example, the rise of AI-driven development may lead to a shift from manually writing large amounts of code to focusing more on designing and optimizing AI models that can generate or improve code automatically. This shift requires a different mindset and a willingness to experiment with new approaches to problem-solving.

Adaptation also extends to organizational culture. Companies that foster a culture of continuous learning and adaptability are better positioned to harness the full potential of AI. This involves creating an environment where learning is encouraged and supported, whether through formal training programs, collaborative learning opportunities, or access to the latest resources and tools. It also means being open to change and innovation, encouraging experimentation, and allowing teams the flexibility to explore new ideas and approaches. By embedding these values into their culture, organizations can ensure that they are not only keeping up with the latest developments but also driving innovation and staying ahead of the competition.

Moreover, continuous learning and adaptation are critical for addressing the evolving demands of users and the market. As AI enables more personalized and responsive software solutions, user expectations are rising. Developers must be able to adapt quickly to changing user needs, incorporating feedback, and iterating on their designs to deliver more effective and satisfying products. This requires a deep understanding of user behavior, as well as the ability to quickly learn and implement new techniques for analyzing and responding to user data.

In conclusion, the need for continuous learning and adaptation in the AI-driven era of software development cannot be overstated. As technology continues to advance at a rapid pace, developers and organizations must remain agile, constantly updating their skills, knowledge, and approaches to stay relevant and competitive. By embracing a mindset of lifelong learning and flexibility, they can not only keep up with the changes but also lead the way in driving innovation and shaping the future of software development. In this ever-changing landscape, the ability to learn and adapt will be the key to success.

Embracing the AI-Powered Future

As we transition into an era increasingly defined by artificial intelligence (AI), embracing the AI-powered future presents both significant opportunities and transformative challenges. The integration of AI into software development and beyond is reshaping industries, driving innovation, and opening new avenues for growth. To fully realize the potential of this new age, individuals and organizations must approach AI with a forward-thinking mindset, ready to adapt, innovate, and leverage its capabilities to drive progress.

At the heart of embracing the AI-powered future is the recognition of AI's potential to enhance efficiency, creativity, and decision-making. AI technologies, such as machine learning, natural language processing, and computer vision, offer unprecedented capabilities for analyzing large datasets, automating complex tasks, and generating insights that were previously out of reach. By integrating AI into their processes, businesses can achieve higher levels of productivity, reduce operational costs, and uncover new opportunities for growth. For instance, AI-driven analytics can provide deeper insights into customer behavior, enabling companies to personalize their offerings and enhance user experiences.

Innovation is a key aspect of embracing the AI-powered future. AI opens the door to novel solutions and applications that were once considered science fiction. From autonomous vehicles and smart cities to advanced healthcare diagnostics and personalized education, AI is driving breakthroughs across diverse fields. Organizations that embrace AI with a spirit of innovation are well-positioned to lead in their industries, creating cutting-edge products and services that meet evolving needs and capitalize on emerging trends. By fostering a culture of experimentation and creativity, businesses can explore new possibilities and push the boundaries of what is achievable with AI.

Adapting to an AI-powered future also involves addressing the ethical and societal implications of AI technology. As AI becomes more prevalent, it is crucial to ensure that its deployment is done responsibly and transparently. This includes addressing issues such as bias in AI models, protecting user privacy, and ensuring that AI systems are used in ways that benefit society as a whole. Embracing the AI-powered future means actively engaging in conversations about ethical considerations, implementing safeguards to prevent misuse, and striving to create AI solutions that are fair, inclusive, and aligned with societal values.

Furthermore, embracing AI involves a commitment to continuous learning and skill development. The rapid advancement of AI technologies means that staying current with new tools, techniques, and best practices is essential. Professionals in the field must be proactive in updating their knowledge and skills, participating in training programs, and staying informed about the latest developments in AI. This ongoing education ensures that individuals and organizations are equipped to harness the full potential of AI and remain competitive in a rapidly evolving landscape.

In addition to individual and organizational efforts, collaboration is key to successfully navigating the AI-powered future. AI is a multidisciplinary field that benefits from diverse perspectives and expertise. By collaborating across industries, academic institutions, and research organizations, stakeholders can share knowledge, address common challenges, and drive collective progress. Partnerships between technology providers, regulators, and community groups can also help shape the development of AI in ways that are beneficial and ethical, ensuring that the technology serves the broader public interest.

Ultimately, embracing the AI-powered future means envisioning and working towards a world where AI enhances human capabilities and improves quality of life. It involves leveraging AI to address pressing global challenges, such as climate change, healthcare accessibility, and economic inequality. By aligning AI development with global goals and values, we can harness its potential to create a more equitable and sustainable future.

In conclusion, embracing the AI-powered future requires a proactive, innovative, and ethical approach. By recognizing the transformative potential of AI, committing to continuous learning, and engaging in responsible development and deployment practices, individuals and organizations can navigate the evolving landscape of AI and drive positive change. As we move forward, the ability to harness AI's capabilities while addressing its challenges will be crucial in shaping a future where technology enhances human progress and well-being.